Joe Schmo Can Catch a Big Fish

Insights from a 61 year old River woman

Joe Schmo Can Catch a Big Fish

Insights from a 61 year old river woman

by Michele White

Joe Schmo Can Catch a Big Fish

Insights from a 61 year old river woman

© 2020 Michele White, Lake George, Colorado

All rights reserved. No part of this book may be reproduced or transmitted in any form or by any means without written permission from the author

"Fishin' is just fishin', am I right?"

(Phil Iwane, 2020)

Contents

INTRODUCTION 1

PART A: THE TRICKS 4

   1. HAVE FAITH: THE TROUT ARE THERE 5

   2. WHAT ARE THE TROUT DOING? 7

   3. KEEP A LOW PROFILE 10

      Sneak, Walk Slowly with Light Footsteps 15

      Dress to Blend 15

      Enter the water 16

   4. DON'T CAST TOO FAR 18

   5. HIT THE FAR BANK 20

      Casting Overhead 21

      Roll Casting 22

      Fly Presentation 24

   6. HIGH-STICK THE LINE 29

   7. THINK LIKE A PUPA 32

      Aquatic Insect Mobility 34

      The Hatch 35

   8. FACE DOWNSTREAM 38

      Flat calm clear water 38

      Skating Over Riffles 41

   9. TUMBLE DRY FLIES UNDERWATER 44

      Drowned terrestrials 44

PART B: SOME DETAILS 45

1. NYMPHING ALL THE WATER 46

Nymphing the Entire Water Column 46

Nymphing Deep Pools 46

Nymphing Shallow Water 47

2. SKATING AND SWINGING 49

Swinging a Nymph pattern 49

Skating a Dry Fly Pattern 51

3. SETTING THE HOOK AND LANDING A BIG FISH 52

Seeing the take 52

The set 53

Let the fish be a fish 56

Get the trout on the reel 56

The final buck 57

The net 58

Landing a trout 58

Unhooking the trout 60

The photo of glory 60

Releasing the Trout 63

PART C: GEAR AND RIGGING 64

1. EQUIPMENT 65

The Rod 65

The Line 66

The Leader and Tippet 67

    Variations on a Theme of Leader, by Haydn (personal bassoonist humor) 69

2.   RIGGING FOR STREAMS: THE POINT FLY AND DROPPER 70

    The Three Painful Knots 71

    The Dry Fly setup 85

    The Nymphing setup 86

    Summary of Michele's Famous Diagram 89

3.   TROUBLE-SHOOTING 90

    Things to Test 90

    Suggestions for Picking Fly Patterns 90

    Big Trout or a Snag? 92

4.   FINAL NOTES 94

ABOUT THE AUTHOR 95

Works Cited 96

APPENDIX I 97

    How to Get Your Line Onto Your Reel: the Backing 97

    How to Connect the Backing to Your Line (painful) 99

    How to Connect the Line to the Leader (if you don't have lovely loops to utilize) 100

INTRODUCTION

You might expect a fishing book to start out describing how to rig the fly rod first and save the more interesting part about catching fish for later. I like the more interesting part first – catching the fish. Then, to keep you on the hook, "How to rig your fly rod" and other useful information, (like knots), are at the end. Yes, there are knots in this book.

Why buy this book? Because this is the best book for Joe Schmo and his wife Shirley. It's simple to read and unique. There are lots of hand-drawn cartoons and illustrations. If you don't like silly insights, you might not like this book. Nearly every day in my fly shop, I commonly tell Joe Schmo (or Shirley) how to catch a big fish in our local waters. We get tons of novice people with a fly rod who have taken and lesson or two and who want to make a go of it on their own. I show them this diagram:

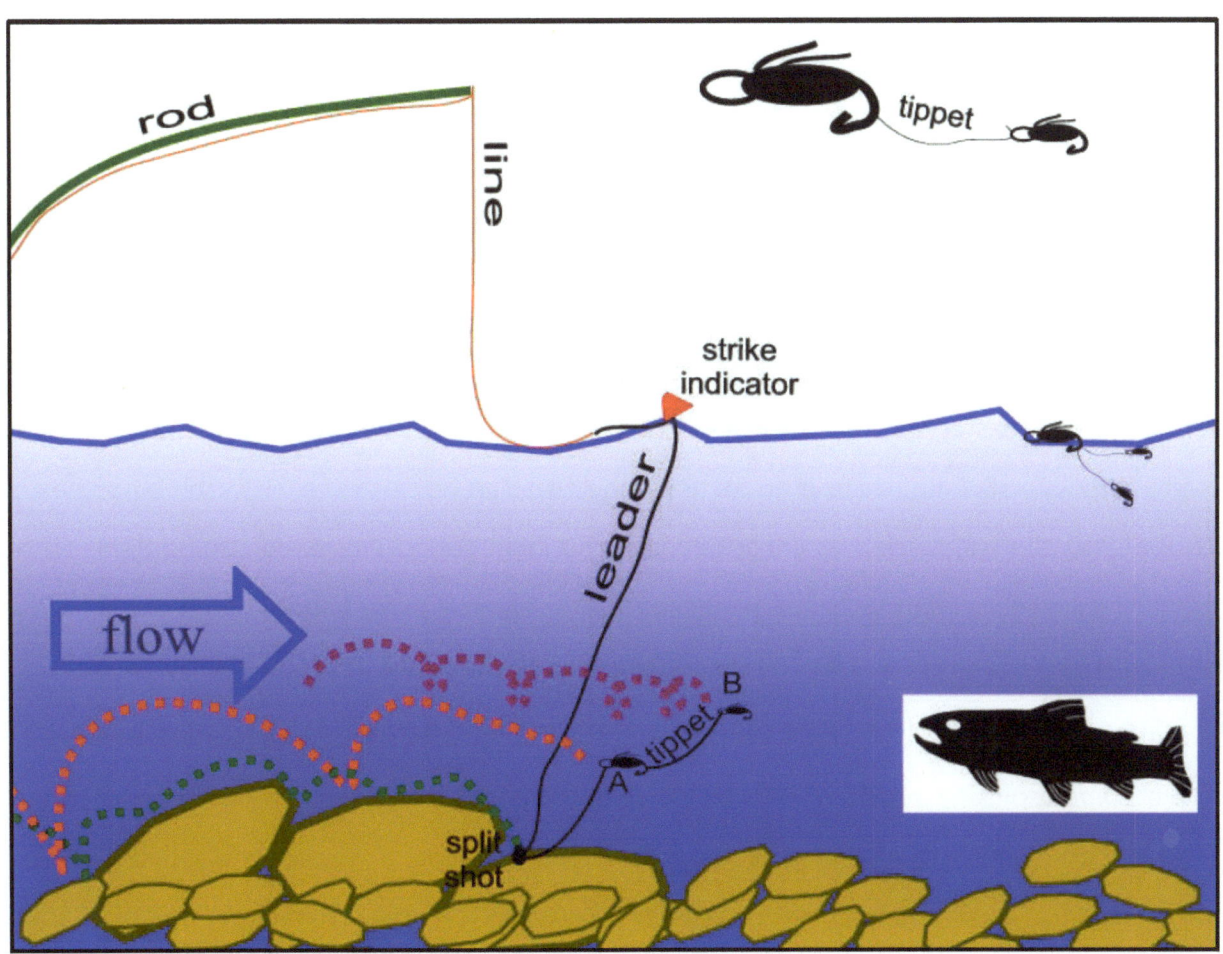

I put their flies on top of the flies in this drawing. I explain what is happening blow-by-blow with the fish and the flies underwater. Then, I send them on their way. They usually come back to tell me how useful this chat was and to show me their fish-on-a-phone. (I get a lot of "fish-on-a-phone" stuck in my face.)

While guiding people who have never been fly fishing before, or who might still be relatively new to the sport, I've noticed a common challenge is that they often don't see the fish, nor do they see the fish's activity (a disturbance on the surface of the water). Even when I point to the ripple or the splash, they still don't see it. I call this ability to see wild animals "wildlife eyes". It's the same experience when I point out a coyote or a deer to someone and they say, "*Where?*" and I point again and say, "*THERE!*" and they still don't see it. I realize some people haven't trained their eyes to detect the telltale shape or movement of a wild animal against the natural backdrop of grass and trees. Same goes for trout spotting. I have pointed and said, *"See that ring on the water? See how there is a circular ripple growing outward, getting bigger? See? That's where a trout stuck its snout or dorsal fin or tail out of the water. That circular ripple on the water is called a 'rise'."* (Sometimes, you can hear the slurp of this event as well if you train your ears to listen for that specific sound.) If a person can't see a ring on the water, then they are really going to have a hard time seeing the shadow of a trout under the water and that makes for a tricky situation for Joe Schmo. Should he give up? NO! He should not give up. He has a lot of tricks he can use to catch a big fish even if he can't see it. (Shirley too!)

I realize it takes time to develop specific skills for fly fishing and I also realize the quandary that Joe Schmo might only have a limited number of hours to catch a fish. He's probably not intending to change his life and become a preeminent fly fishing master, (though, he just might. One never knows where life's passion will lead you.) Not today, though. Today, Joe Schmo has four hours to catch a fish that he can't see. This isn't a hopeless situation. Have heart, Joe! You can still catch a wily trout even if you can't see it. This book should give you some easy tactics for catching a wily trout in technical water (by that, I mean a picky fish in a high-use area, such as we have here in South Park, Colorado at Eleven Mile Canyon and the Dream Stream.)

I decided to put my daily advice in writing, starting the book with walking up to the stream and fishing, then putting the parts about picking a rod and selecting flies at the end. That may seem out of order but that's how I operate: I go and do things first. Afterward, I seek the details. Joe Schmo can take the rod he just bought (he'll call it a pole for a while) from a general sporting goods store and if he reads the first chapter of this book, he may have a good chance at catching a fish. Maybe even a big fish.

Here are the systematic means to achieving this goal:

- HAVE FAITH: THE TROUT ARE THERE
- WHAT ARE THE TROUT DOING
- KEEP A LOW PROFILE
- DON'T CAST TOO FAR
- CAST TO THE FAR BANK
- HIGH-STICK THE LINE
- THINK LIKE A PUPA
- FACE DOWNSTREAM
- TUMBLE DRY FLIES UNDERWATER

(There - that's *IT*! Now, you don't need to read the book.)

If you do read this book, you'll peruse details on how to land a big fish, my opinions of equipment, and instructions for rigging your line for the stream. That last part, rigging for the stream, in itself is really useful – painful because it includes knots – but useful because of the color illustrations.

Thank you for buying this book,

Michele White

PART A: THE TRICKS

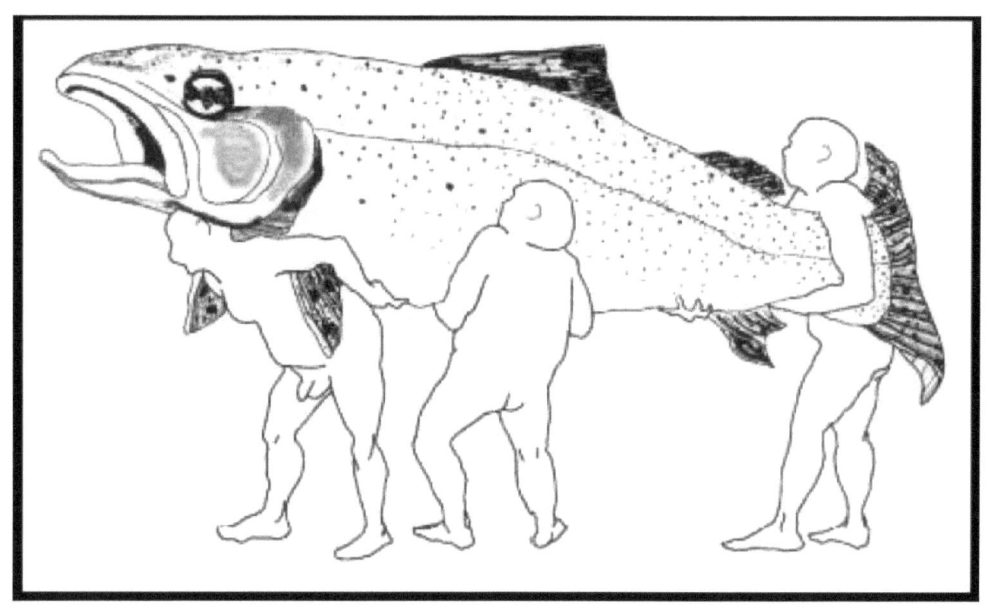

1. HAVE FAITH: THE TROUT ARE THERE

In a high-use area, such as Eleven Mile Canyon or the Dream Stream in Colorado, you might be surprised to know how many fish are just hanging out near you waiting for you to leave. The fish see a lot of humans and they've learned that if they hunker down and don't feed for a while that you will probably give up. Right? If you are not catching any fish and you don't see any fish activity, you will leave. That's pretty clever of a trout, isn't it? That's not normally how a trout would behave, though. On most any other wild stream (one that is not controlled by dams or barriers) the wild trout seldom see people and they're afraid of us. Normally, trout have options for places to flee. Wild trout will scatter like mice when you approach the water. They skedaddle making zigzags running over each other to get away from you[1]. Oddly, this isn't usually the case in a high-use area like a Gold Medal[2] water. There are a lot of reasons, (not solely due to the fish being used to people), for fish in a Gold Medal habitat to hang out rather than flee. A big factor is that the trout are confined within a limited run of a couple miles with few options for fleeing. They don't have anywhere better to go. Their habitat is only a mile or two long. They know there are humans upstream and downstream. They have learned that if they just hang out and don't feed for a while, you will move on. That is an educated fish.

NOTEWORTHY: Trout notice things and they remember events, both good and bad experiences.

In our region (South Park, Colorado – a 9,000 feet high altitude basin between mountain ranges), we have multiple Gold Medal waters. Two of these areas are "tailwater" systems – places where the spillway below a dam drains from the bottom of the reservoir and therefore is usually of a consistent, cool but not freezing temperature and is well oxygenated. Water spilling over the top of a dam is derived from the surface of a reservoir, which is susceptible to temperature variations with the season. Water that comes out of the bottom of a reservoir is – NOT FROZEN. So, a tailwaters released from the bottom of a dam is fishable year round – IT DOESN'T FREEZE. The most significant aspect of a tailwater that never freezes, is that the aquatic insects are

---

[1] Of note: I have a theory that scared fish either emit a pheromone or a sound, like a croak when they are frightened. I say this because of the way other fish become alerted when one of them is terrified. Even way upstream or downstream, one terrified fish means they all become nervous.

[2] Gold Medal Waters are the highest quality cold-water habitats for fish and have the capability to hold many quality-size (14 inches or longer) trout. Gold Medal Waters are defined as any river or lake which is producing a standing stock of at least 60 pounds per acre, and at least 12 trout that are 14 inches or longer per acre on a sustained basis. River segments designated as Gold Medal Trout Waters must be a minimum of 2 miles in length, and lakes must be a minimum of 50 acres. (Colorado State Parks & Wildlife Office, 2018)

constantly engaged in their lifecycle of reproduction and generating more pupae[3] or nymphs, which are a trout's main diet.

Mysis shrimp[4] and / or scuds[5] (crustacean species of little aquatic animals) are often artificially introduced to tailwaters by state biologists to provide super enriched nutrition (power food) for sustaining huge trout. The spillway area provides the cool temperature and elevated oxygen levels (water flowing and frothing down a spillway picks up free oxygen as it splashes) that these populations of freshwater crustaceans thrive on. These particular crustacean species are commonly added to tailwaters in order to feed the growing population of fat trout that are living like couch potatoes at spillways. Crustaceans and abundant pupae and nymphs are why trout get so big in a tailwater. A permanent population of huge trout is how a tailwater becomes classified as Gold Medal. That is why Joe Schmo needs to know about and look for tailwaters in his region for fly fishing.

> *NOTEWORTHY: If you are ever trapped alive having to stay in a place you don't want to visit, go get a map. Look for local dams and find out which flow from the bottom. Chances are, there may be a fishable tailwaters for you to escape from your situation.

Point being, when you are in a high-use area like a tailwater, the trout are likely to hold in place. They are hanging out waiting for you to leave because their habitat is a limited area and they have no place to go. Your job is to out-wait them. Take your time. Be conservative in your movements. They are going to stay put. Have faith: trout are there.

---

[3] Did you know that the insects you see flying around the stream have been living in the water as pupae for maybe a year or more? The adult stage is so short that some species don't even have functional mouths in the adult form!

[4] Mysids are not true shrimp. They don't have a free-swimming larval phase. Female mysid carry up to 30 developing young in a pouch at the base of their legs. As soon as the fry develop, they go free into the water and the female prepares a new batch of eggs. Mysis shrimp reach adult size (1 inch) in about 3 weeks, this leads to a new generation being created every 30 days. (Ulrich, III, 2018)

[5] Scuds (means "side-swimmers") are freshwater invertebrates belonging to the order Amphipoda. The name "side-swimmer" comes from the way these animals swim. Scuds are omnivores and eat any organic material they come upon. They live in both flowing and still waters. They crawl at the bottom or swim on their sides. Their body length ranges from 5 - 20 mm (without antennae). There is no separate larval stage - young look like small adults and become sexually mature after growing and shedding their skin several times. (Hamrsky, 2018)

2. WHAT ARE THE TROUT DOING?

Observing trout behavior on the surface of the water definitely helps you select the right fly but recognizing why a trout is acting that way also helps you decide what to do next. There are different methods of presenting a fly to a trout. Joe can catch a big fish on a stream using two basic methods: fishing on the surface of the water with dry flies, or fishing under the water using nymph patterns. By the way, this topic, (methods of fly fishing) is where fishermen will go on and on and have a lot to say about their personal experience. Discussing methods of fly fishing can be enlightening and enjoyable but it can also be exhausting. There are certainly many different, creative methods to choose from for fly fishing but the two I am proposing here are the most common methods that work well enough. That is why I am writing this book: easy non-complicated fly fishing.

Let's talk about what you might see on the surface, because you may not have the skills to see trout activity under the water yet. Trout do different things that are visible to us on the surface. Most commonly, they feed on the surface by sipping in a line of oncoming insects that are drifting in the current. The trout might be hovering just below the surface and intermittently rising to suck a floating insect down. The trout might be holding kind of still in a lair, like hanging out against a boulder or under an overhanging back. They might alternate between rising to take an oncoming insect and then swiftly return to their lair. This kind of feeding is usually consistent and if you watch them, you can time your cast to the intermittence of their next rise. Sometimes trout "tool around" kind of trolling with their mouths open to vacuum the surface in a calm eddy or pool (they have to be feeling fairly secure to do this). Alternatively, trout might only hit on the surface for a one time opportunistic chance. The opportunistic trout is not as reliable a target as the intermittent eater. Then, there are the spectacular breaches that capture our attention. I've found that when I see trout coming completely out of the water like a missile, they are either...

- piercing through the path of an ascending emerging insect, (observing this behavior indicates it is a good time to use a pupae-emerging adult pattern and give the fly a little action by twitching it or letting the fly swing in the current); or
- the trout is grabbing a hovering adult insect clean out of the air *BANG!!*; or
- the trout is happy (trout get frisky, especially pre-spawn adults and spunky juveniles); or
- the trout is fleeing from an underwater predator like a pike.

WHAT ARE THE TROUT DOING?

When fly fishing a common high country stream in the Rocky Mountains (Colorado, Wyoming, Montana, Idaho, Utah, and New Mexico), you can usually walk up to a normal stream and fling some flashy pattern like a Royal Wulff[6] into the water and catch a proper fish. One fly. Easy. Not on a technical water, though. In a tailwater, you are going to need two flies regardless if you are dry fly fishing or nymphing: the first fly is to attract the trout and the second fly is for the trout to pick up as an afterthought when he rejects the first fly. (Some people use 3 flies. That's too much gear to control for Joe and you've just tripled the money a snag will cost.)

Whether you are dry fly fishing or nymphing, there is a basic premise to presenting a fly to a trout. Remember: trout are always facing into the current (which is usually upstream unless the eddy is making the water flow backwards, in which case a trout will be facing downstream into the current). Trout are lining up on potential snacks drifting in the current to their lair. You need a fly that is going to make their ears perk up – an attention getter. Joe needs to put this fly in the exact line of oncoming debris that the trout is feeding on. The fly needs to be upstream when it first enters the trout's vision (about 8 feet upstream). The chow line isn't a simple straight line in front of a trout, either. Watch the debris and foam on the surface to see the path of floating stuff. The chow line may be a little to the left or right of the trout when it is upstream and then get deflected over to the trout. Conversely, the oncoming fly you set directly in front of a feeding trout might get deflected away from the trout before it reaches the trout. Watch the hydraulics and put your fly in the seam that feeds directly into the trout's nose.

---

[6] Wulff is not wolf. Lee Wulff (February 10, 1905 – April 28, 1991), born Henry Leon Wulff, was an artist, pilot, fly fisherman, author, filmmaker, outfitter and conservationist who made significant contributions to recreational fishing, especially fly fishing and the conservation of Atlantic Salmon. He was married 4 times....his last wife, Joan Salvato Wulff, also known as the "First Lady of Fly Fishing", is widely regarded as the architect of modern-day fly-casting mechanics. He died in a plane crash. Joan is still contributing to our world.

WHAT ARE THE TROUT DOING?

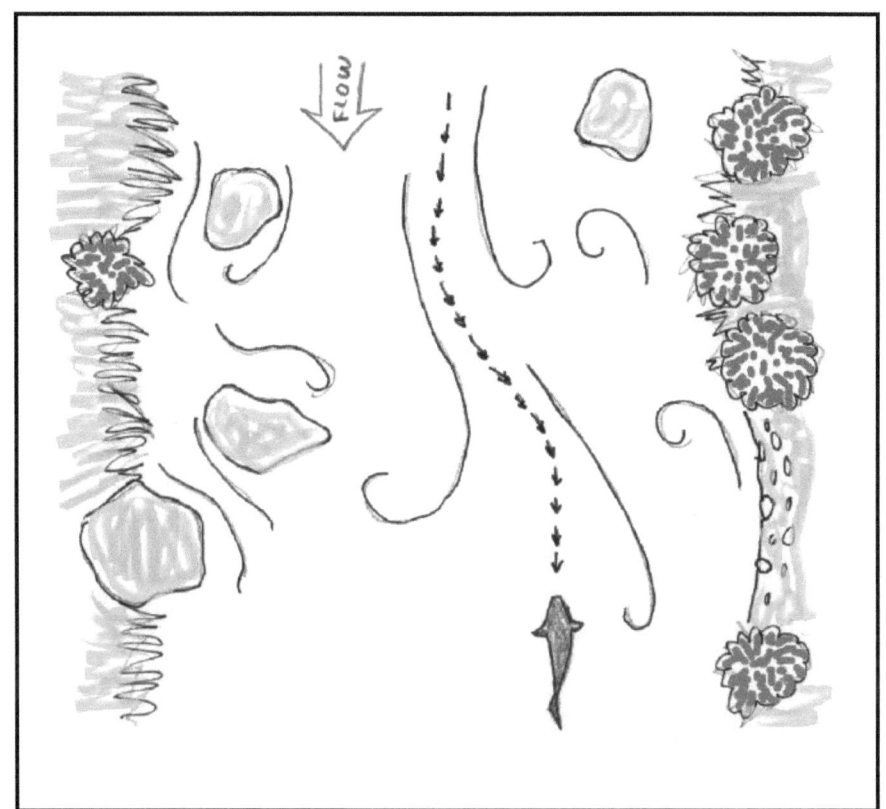

Figure 1 Deflected line of food coming to a trout.

3. KEEP A LOW PROFILE

No matter what method you are chose to start fishing (dry fly on the surface or nymphing underwater), you need to be stealthy. Both your approach to the water and your position in the water need to keep your profile below the horizon. That is because of how trout see things.

Trout see in a cone of vision above them. If you keep under the angle of their vision, you can creep up on them without them being able to see you. (Though they can feel the thumping of your boots if you tread heavily and hear your voice if you are talking loudly.)

> *DIGRESSION – Trout eyes have both rods and cones. They can see color, ultraviolet, and even polarized light (can see though glare). They focus their eyes by moving the lens closer or further from the retina. Plus, the eyes focus independently in almost every direction simultaneously. That is a pretty darn sophisticated eyeball, (Coughlin & Hawryshyn, 1994).*

Sight is the ability for optical nerves in an eyeball to sense light waves (bands of photons) and send a message to the brain, which interprets that stimulation as an image (stay with me here, I won't digress too far). The speed of light waves makes different colors and is affected by passing through different mediums (textures), such as air or water. (Ever watch the moon rise really huge on the horizon and then it gets smaller in the sky? That is a phenomenon of seeing the moon through thicker atmosphere at a low angle and then through thinner atmosphere at a higher angle.) Point being of that point being, is when we look at a fish the light waves of the fish we are seeing are passing through two mediums – air and then water – before arriving in our eyeball. That goes vice versa for the fish. When a fish is looking up at the surface of the water to see what is on the bank, it sees light through two mediums – water and air. The result to both viewers is a bent (refracted) image, like this:

 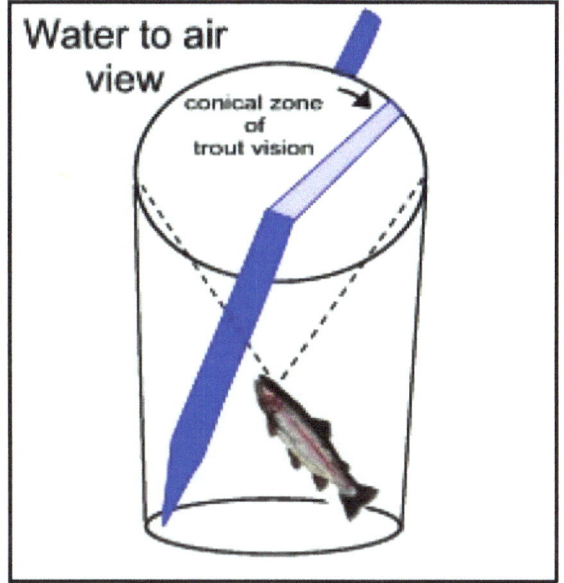

The "thing" you are looking at underwater is not in the location you think it is. It's actually located a little bit downward – a bent view. We look down through air and into the water but the true location of the pencil (or fish) is actually bent downward a bit. A fish looking up at us can only see the part of us that is in its field of view due to the bank limiting the surface of the water. Plus, what the fish sees is bent to the side. They can't see the part that is deflected out of view.

Here is a more basic look at this concept:

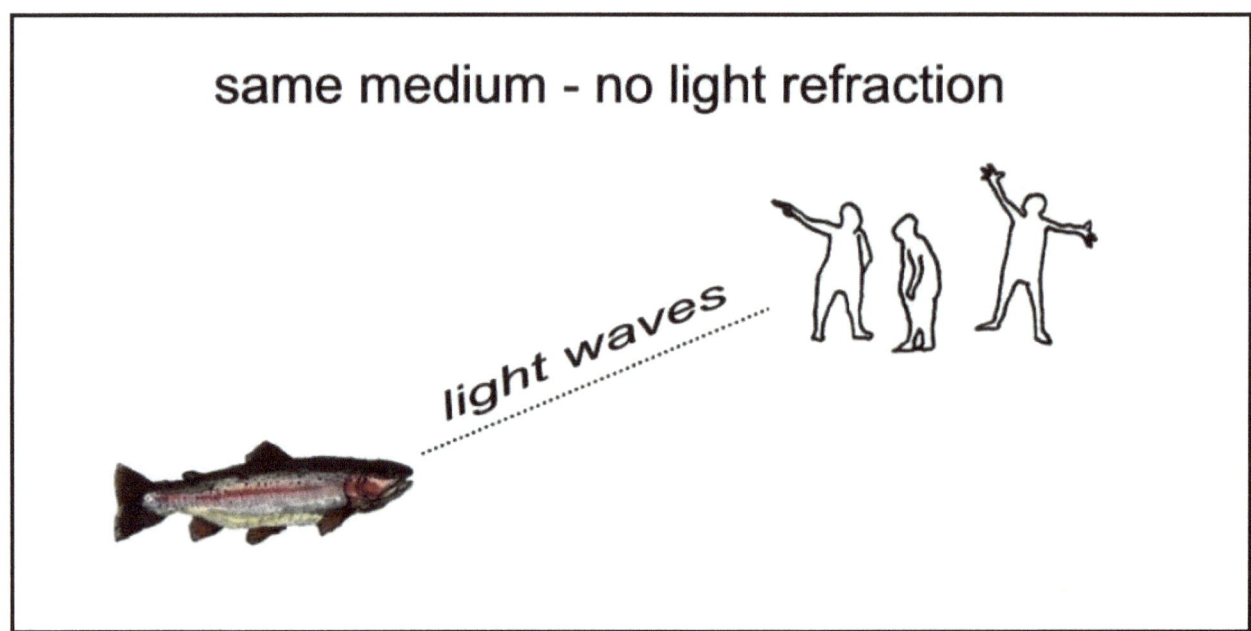

If there was no water, (or if we were underwater) we and the trout would see each other equally. But when we are in the air and the trout is in the water, we each are seeing each other in a "bent" view. The trout has a blind spot because we are on the bank. Because of the bank, a trout's vision is limited to the water's surface *AND* the image it sees is bent (refracted) to the side. The result is a pretty big blind spot on the bank to a trout.

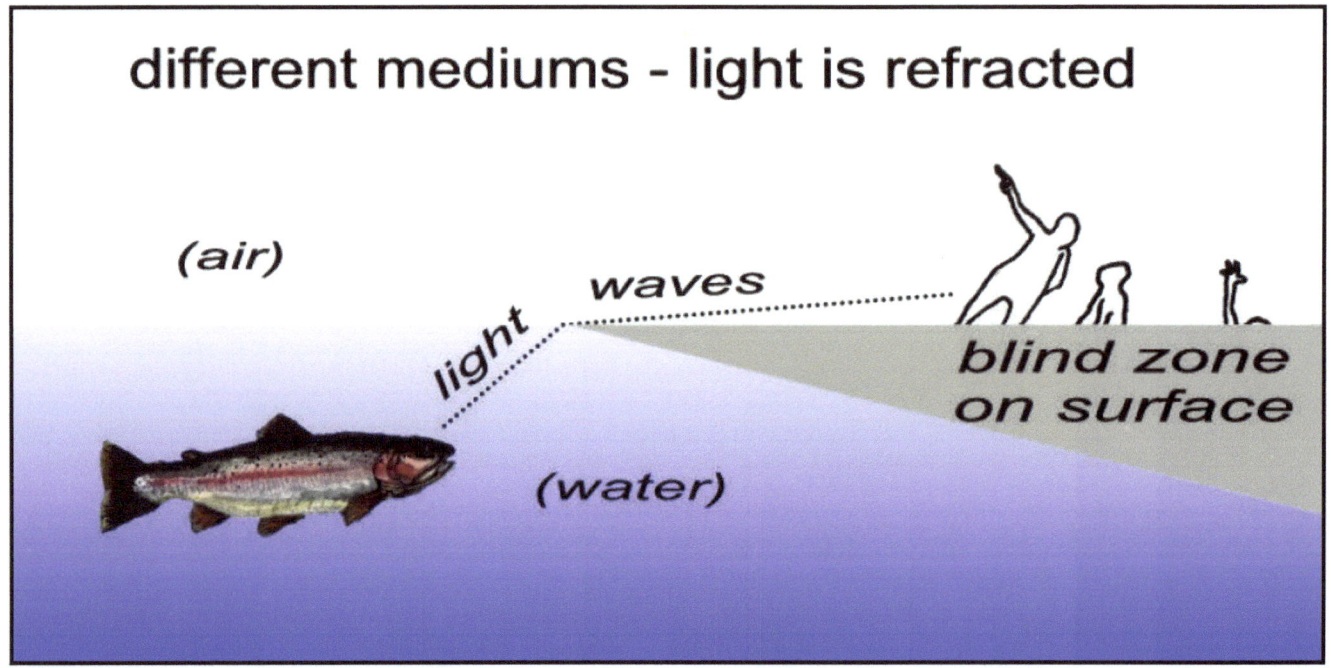

Consequently, you can avoid a trout's cone of visibility by staying within its blind spot, which is low to the ground.

Figure 2 Joe Schmo and his dog Elmo at the bank.

Figure 3 Distortion due to riffles.

Figure 4 water-to-air distortion deflects the imagery.

Figure 5 The trout only sees part of what is on the bank – cannot see the shorter guy on the right.

KEEP A LOW PROFILE

Thusly, here are some generalized tips for approaching the water that you intend to fish at:

SNEAK, WALK SLOWLY WITH LIGHT FOOTSTEPS

There are often deep undercuts in the bank underneath your footstep and you are literally walking on the ceiling of the trout's safe place. Lower your voice. Keep your arms and gear close to your body and move with conservation. Bend over, hunker down. Get shorter as you get near the stream. Kneel on a knee to look at the stream and make a plan for your first cast based on what you see. Notice the character of the water. Are there runs[7], riffles, boulders, deep pools, shallow zones?

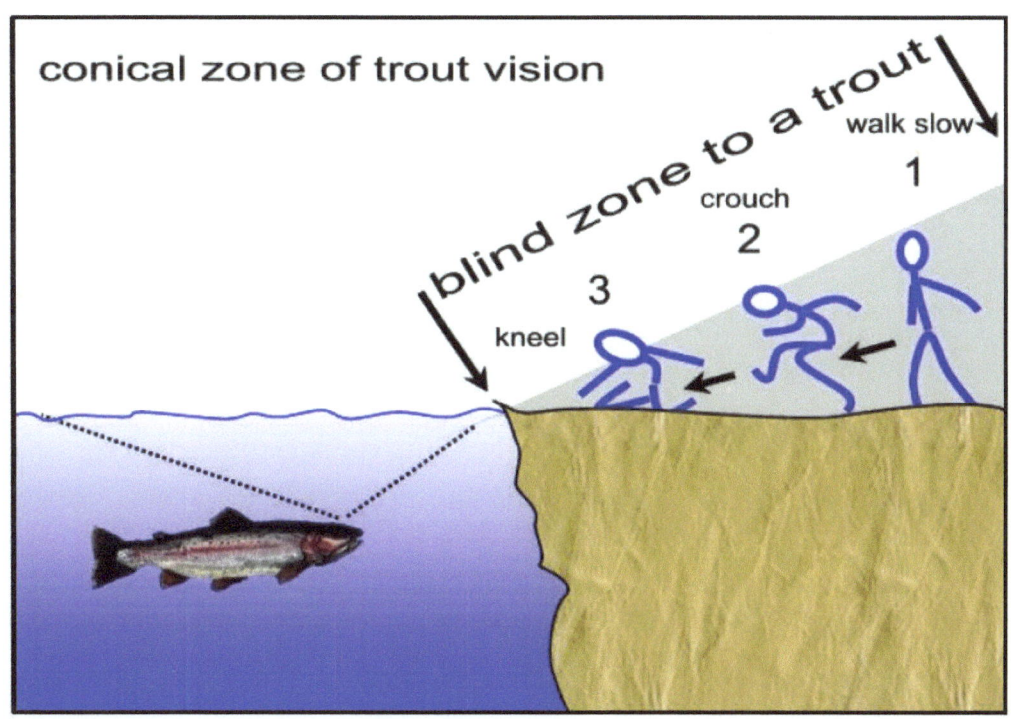

DRESS TO BLEND

Are you in a grassy or bushy area? Are you in a rocky canyon? Are you on a barren plain with the sky behind you? Dress to blend in with the background. At the least, avoid bright colors. No bright shirts or hats or reflective mirrored glasses. Of course, the trout are going to see you eventually, but to what degree are you going to alarm this creature? Can he tolerate you or are you frightening?[8] Wear earth-tone clothes. Avoid clothing with large

---

[7] A run is the stream flowing fairly straight and smooth with some depth to the channel; a riffle is the stream flowing over a shallow area with cobbles on the floor and the top of the water is lumpy and bumpy.

[8] I have the personal opinion that trout may recognize people, especially a recurring person fishing the same hole every day. Trout recall you. "Oh, here comes that thin guy in the blue baseball hat again." Change your hat.

graphics. If you wear bright orange, you will have to utilize superior powers to wrangle a trout. The trout look upward for two reasons: A) to look for a snack; and B) to watch for predators. Are you a predator? Yes, you are! Approach the water with stealth.

ENTER THE WATER

By now, you have snuck to the water's edge and are kneeling on one knee wearing your beige or camo fishing pants and light-colored fly fishing shirt and a low profile cream-colored hat. Your rod is held *pointing behind* you away from the water and not waving around up in the sky. You have evaluated the stream in front of you and made a plan of action. When I first approach the bank (bending lower as I approach), I make a plan for where I want to cast based on what I see: target #1, target #2, etc. I start by dropping my fly to the closest target on the water, which is usually just over the side of the bank. I might hang my line over the bank and blindly drift my fly on the surface of the water in case there is a fish there. I slowly skim my fly as close to the bank I am kneeling on. This is a very effective way to pick up a large lunker who has no clue a human has arrived. In this way, I have "sterilized" that portion of real estate nearest to me and I can now swing my legs over and enter the water. You can also start by sitting on a boulder or maybe sitting on the bank dangling your feet over the edge.

It is now time to get in the water. Why? Because the trout need to settle down and you should lower your profile off the sky as much as possible. Find a place you can get into the water without making a splash. Pick a place to stand where you can utilize a backdrop – a cliff, a wall of willows, a structure of some kind. If you keep your profile within the silhouette of a larger profile behind you, then your presence is more obscure to a trout than if the trout sees you standing against the horizon hovering like a blue heron.

Wait until you are in the water with your feet firmly planted before you cast to your planned target. The fish will notice you by now. They know you are there. They will just hang out keeping an eye on you and not feed. The trout are waiting for you to leave. You can out-wait a trout by taking time to tie and nip your tippet to make dropper-tag extensions, peruse your flies. All this time, the trout is just waiting for you to leave. You will win this waiting game. It's not that hard.

> *"Juvenile trout are curious. They want to investigate. They want to look at new and interesting stuff. People are something new, something interesting to think about. However, they are wary of you."*

This moment of repose is an interesting point in time. We have both trout and human hunkered down committed to the stay. Who is going to lose their concentration first? I tell you: the trout will lose this test. Trout are not known for their patience. Trout have no self-discipline when it comes to wanting to graze. They will resume feeding with skepticism once they decide you are not a threat.

> *"A trout wants to believe that people are no threat, though it will always be leery of being grabbed and eaten by you."*

4. DON'T CAST TOO FAR

By this point, you are standing in the water (or sitting on a rock). You've rigged your line according to the method you have decided on using (surface fishing with a dry fly or sub-surface fishing by nymphing) and you have made an initial plan for where you want to cast first. WHY IN THE WORLD WOULD YOU WANT TO TRY AND CAST 50-FEET UPSTREAM? You just got settled with the trout. They are not startled anymore and they are starting to graze again. The trout are all around you, keeping an eye on you, undulating to the left, to the right, a little up and then back down again, munching on tiny midge pupae that are floating in the current like underwater fairy dust. Tell me why you are casting (trying to cast) with rigor and verve so far upstream? The action of false casting riles the trout just as they were getting used to your presence. Your waving arm and rod, the colored line overhead - all this action makes them nervous. Mending the line makes a plucking sound, which makes them nervous. Some people false cast repeatedly, reloading the line on the water and picking up to cast again and again until they finally "feel" like they've got the fly just where they want it. That effort takes up time. Meanwhile, all the trout in your area have decided that you are dangerous. Guess what they did about that? You didn't notice, but they lifted their bodies into the current and let the stream carry them downstream away from you. If you look upstream all the fish are gone. Turn around. They're behind you now, downstream, jostling for a cozy place behind your feet so they can feed on the pupae that you have been kicking up.

> *On the San Juan River in New Mexico at the tailwater below Navajo Dam, this trout behavior (stacking up behind your feet) is so pervasive that the trout might tap on your boots with their snouts to get you to scoot your feet. This is known as the San Juan Shuffle. Stirring up the sediments with pupae deliberately to attract trout is considered bad form in the angling world. Don't do it. We won't invite you anymore.*

There are very few streams in Colorado that you need to cast more than 20 feet. Ever. Casting out of an anchored drift boat to access a long line of feeding trout on a river is one example of needing to cast far. Casting across a huge placid bend where the stream bulges out into a large pool like below Taylor Reservoir is another. Wade fishing on a lake means casting far, too (but maybe not). Otherwise, on most common streams you can cast to the far side within 30 feet. If you do cast way upstream, your line will put down all the fish between you and your distant fly. That is a lot of fish to frighten.

There are perfectly nice fish near you. They are hanging out in pocket water[9] behind boulders, under overhanging bushes, lying in the shadow against the bank, or nestled between imbricated cobbles in a riffle run because the riffles make a bumpy surface and a predator can't see them there in between the rocks. All that these fish are doing is opening and closing their mouths (aspiration with their gills) and toggling their sophisticated eyeballs around to watch for predators and to keep track of other fish (fish have friends). Most significantly, though, trout are always watching-watching-watching upstream for "The Trigger".

A trout's trigger is a tumbling speck in the water column that has a size and shape of a snack that they like. They watch as The Trigger approaches. They notice details, such as movement. Is it a squiggling, undulating pupa / nymph or a dead drift particle of debris? Is it an artificial fly with an unnatural drag? Is it tumbling in a linear path toward them or is it drifting away? Ideally, a trout's trigger will start to look like something they recognize as it gets closer. They will identify an insect's thorax, tail, budding wing sack and gills. Ideally, their potential snack will be drifting toward them in the current directly upstream so they can line up and time their take. They won't chase after it. All a trout wants to do is to tilt one fin and bend its head over to the side to pick the insect out of the current with its mouth and then tilt the fin again to return to its comfortable lair facing upstream to look at the rest of the oncoming detritus in the water. Minimal effort. That's the trout's motto.

> *Older large trout are simply underwater couch potatoes. They rarely chase after their snack, certainly not for a midge pupa. Juvenile trout will get frisky and play with their food, play with debris, play with each other – even bother the larger fish by picking on them and darting around like scamps. The larger trout are bothered by this fun and sometimes move off to get away from the pesky rascals until the youngsters simmer down. When a large trout is in the mood to be a predator, though, all the other fish know. Maybe there is a pheromone involved, but the behavior of a predatory trout has an impact on the behavior of other fish. A large predatory trout is a dangerous buddy. Trust me: trout know each other.*

Joe Schmo needs to keep his cast close, keep the colored part of the line off the water as much as possible and cast to the nearest pocket water. This single action is the number one change-up in methodology for catching a wily trout in a technical water: cast closer to you and present the fly to the most effective area.

THERE – THAT IS A BIG CLUE IN JOE SCHMO CATCHING A BIG FISH IN TECHNICAL WATER!

---

[9] Pocket: an underwater spot where the current is slow, such as behind a boulder. The current will swing around an obstacle, which creates a pressure shadow where the water is deflected. There are pockets of soft current where the flow is deflected.

5. HIT THE FAR BANK

Before you leave the spot where you have been presenting your fly to a targeted pocket water, you have to cast for the far bank. The easiest way to get your fly all the way across the stream with stealth is to pull enough line off the reel to cover that distance before you cast. Let the excess line drop in the water at your feet and hold a reserve of it loosely in your free hand. Another option in preparation for a good far cast across the stream, is to point the rod downstream and wiggle the tip, pumping it to feed line out. Let the stream pull the excess line downstream – a length of the distance across the stream plus about 10 feet extra. Think about your cast before you execute. You should be aiming for about 45^0 upstream and across the water from where you are standing. If you have pulled line off the reel and it is laying in the water at your feet, you will have to false cast to get the line fully extended up in the air. If the line is extended downstream, you will have to lower the tip of the rod and time your lift with care so that the line doesn't make a tell-tell sucking sound when you pull free of the water. This latter method you will just pull the line out of the water and lob it upstream - no false casting. Lift and lob.

So, you are planning the cast in your mind's eye. Prior to casting, get in position by pointing your feet 45^0 upstream. Rather than destroying your element of surprise with a sloppy presentation to the target (*PLOP!*), maybe work your way to the target by casting halfway to your target and letting that cast drift downstream. Work your way closer. All casts should be about 45^0 upstream but targeting further out in the water each time. Your eventual goal is to get your fly against the far bank. The first shorter casts have sterilized the water between you and the far bank. There might be a fish between you and the far bank. You don't want to miss that opportunity by casting across the stream and draping the fish in the middle of the stream with your line.

Each time you cast, you let a little more line out. By the time you have cast 3-4 times, the line is long enough to reach the far side. That is where the big trout are: on the far bank, just about touching the bank, lying in wait for your fly to come. They are waiting for this snack from a lair hiding under an overhanging part of the bank[10].

There is no such thing as a bad cast. If the fly is on the water - a fish can get it. If it is in the air being whipped around until some brain cell says, *"COMMIT-COMMIT!!"* all a trout can do is roll over laughing (or leave from embarrassment). When I look at the water, I like to divide it up in my mind into chunks of real estate making a plan of assault starting with the closest water for Target #1 and reserving the furthest water for subsequent

---

[10] I've seen trout using a fin or their tail touching the bank or a rock to keep themselves steady in a lair: conservation of energy.

casts. The far bank is the goal. You should approach that cast with practice and get a feeling for the wind, the sun glare, and any other environmental effects on your cast before you land your fly on the far bank.

CASTING OVERHEAD

Something to understand about your overhead cast is the elasticity of the line itself. That is, the line is designed to s-t-r-e-t-c-h for a lingering moment <u>behind you</u> up in the air before it will recoil in a soft ricochet to shoot forward. It's that stretching that bends the rod (loads the rod) and prepares the recoil to operate like an atlatl (… yes, an atlatl). In order to get your line to stretch and extend and reach further, you must wait - actually come to a stop – between your back-cast and your forward-cast. Literally, stop in the sky and wait for your line to stretch out behind you. Don't tip your rod way back. Stop the tip in the air by your ear. Only the line goes back. Once the line has extended behind you and flattened out into a tight flat loop then, it will come ricocheting forward like a rubber band. The timing is

… back cast ⊢ *wait* ⊣ … forward cast ⊢ *wait* ⊣ … back cast ⊢ *wait* ⊣ … forward cast ⊢ *wait* ⊣ …

like a clock: tick……tock……tick……tock.

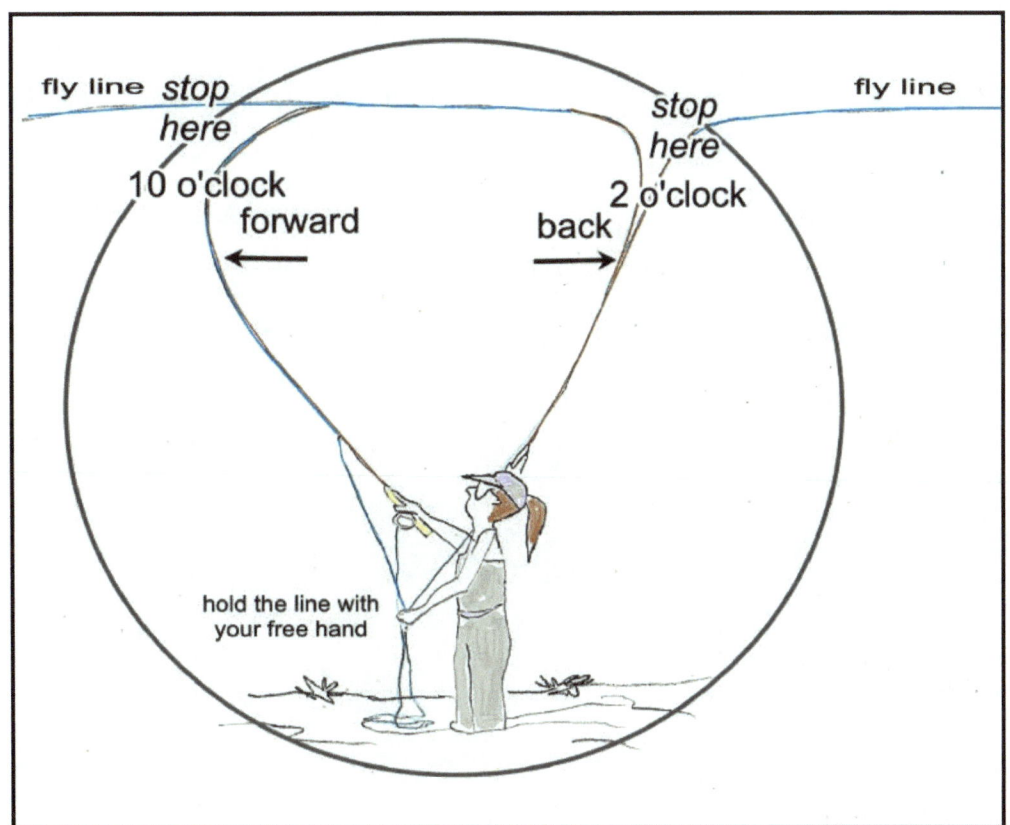

Figure 60 Overhead Cast: stopping at 10 o'clock and 2 o'clock.

Give yourself TIME between the casts going backwards and forwards. If you look up at the line, you should see it making a flat loop above your head, not a big arch in the sky. Tilt your head back and look up at the line – turn your face up and watch what your line is doing. The exact place to stop the rod mid-air is at 10 o'clock, which feels like right in front of your face, and 2 o'clock, right beside your ear. I swear if you just wait about two seconds and count "one…two" between your back-cast and when you cast forward again, you will feel the sensation of the line stretching and you will see the line go way farther forward than you have ever cast before. You increase your extension by allowing the line to stretch hard and then recoil, rather than by dropping the rod behind you and tossing the line forward like a dirty old sock. You only want to cast to the other side of the stream anyway. So, you only need to cast about 20 feet. To cast further distance, stop your swing in the air and let the line really stretch *BEHIND YOU*….

Roll Casting

Your most effective cast is not the overhead "Brad-Pitt-A-River-Runs-Through-It" cast. Joe Schmo's most effective cast is a basic roll-cast. Pull the line across water next to you skimming the surface. Then, flip the rod tip forward. This pulls the line off the surface of the water in a progression, which makes a spiral loop moving across the water. You can start a roll cast by flicking some excess line out onto the water by wiggling the tip back and forth to drop ziggy zaggy loops on the water. Slowly pull the line alongside of you letting it glide on the surface of the water with your rod held out to the side and a little behind you (not overhead). This makes the ziggy-zaggy loops straighten out a bit, too. Then stop pulling. When you stop pulling, the line will slow down and soften into some slack. At that moment, you flick the tip forward and up, which causes the line to lift off the water and roll out across the water. This is a very effective cast to avoid getting hung up on bushes behind you because there is no back cast. NO BACK CAST!!

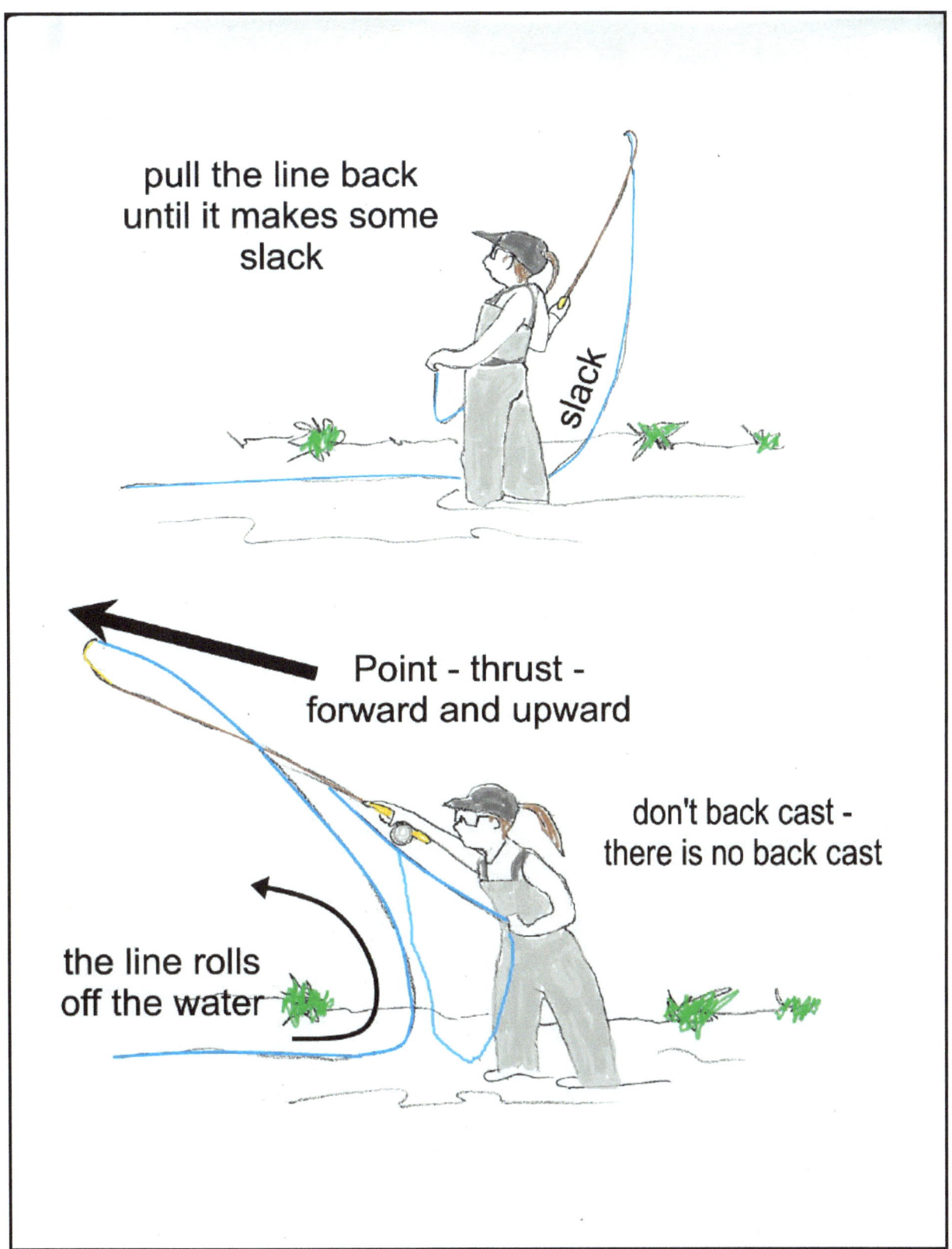

Figure 7 Yer basic roll cast.

Fly Presentation

You need to cast your fly a few feet upstream of the desired target so that a trout has time to watch it, think about it, and then line up on it. When you are ready to cast, <u>don't</u> aim for a spot on the water. Aim about 4 feet <u>above the water</u> and let the line shoot out to its maximum extension <u>up in the air</u>. Follow the line and fly with the rod tip as the fly sinks down to the surface of the water like fairy dust. This is done softly. The fly drifting on the surface of the water down to the trout lair needs to be dead still with no action (except for specific insect species to be discussed later...).

Keep your lowered rod tip pointed at the fly all the time. Get ready for action immediately.

Once the fly is on the water you must immediately initiate some kind action to compensate for the moving current. The water in the center of the stream moves faster downstream than the water along the margins (a phenomenon of friction against the bank). To keep the fly from being pulled unnaturally fast downstream by the line, you have to "mend" (lift portions of the fly line gently off the water and flick parts of the fly line upstream). Mending will allow the line to move downstream at the same rate at which the fly is drifting downstream. You will continually be mending the line upstream until the fly eventually sinks or is pulled under the water – ideally that occurs downstream of your target.

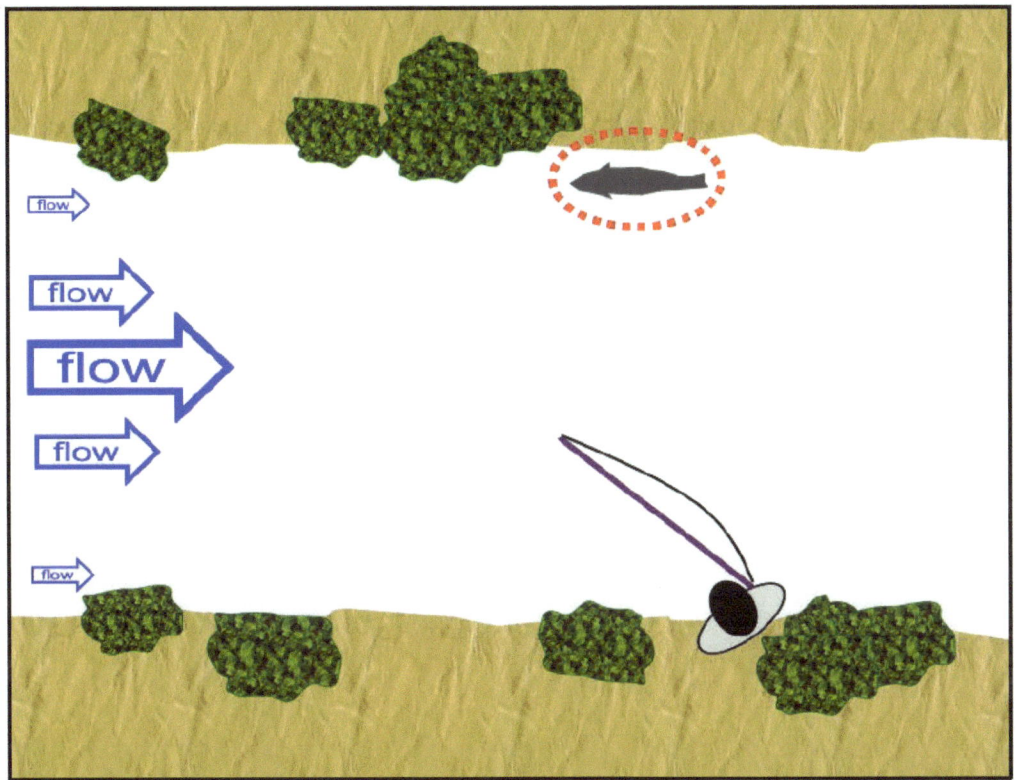

Figure 8 Joe thinks there should be a proper fish downstream of that bush on the far bank.

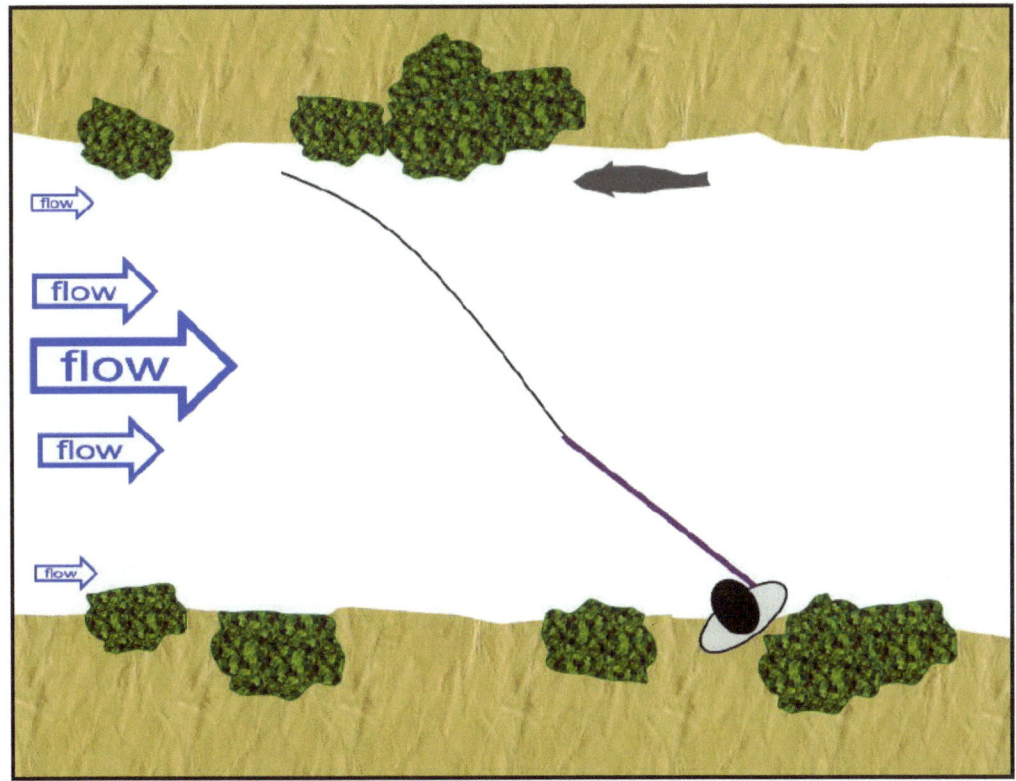

Figure 9 Joe casts about 45^0 upstream above the suspected fish.

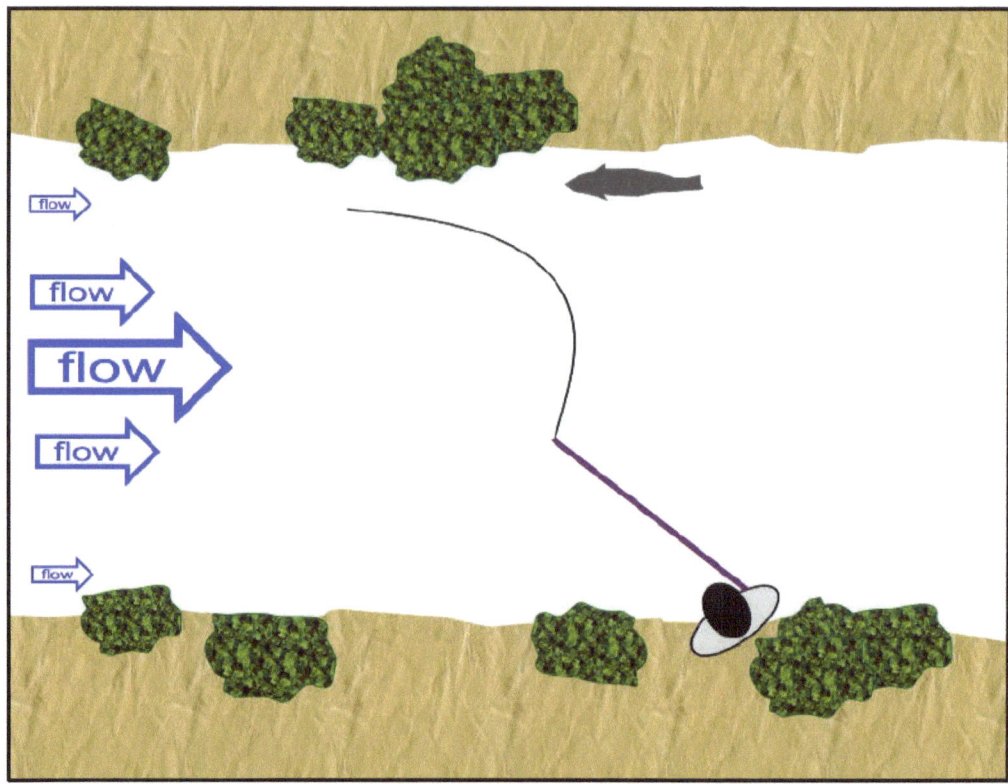

Figure 10 Dang! The current immediately pulls Joe's line downstream faster than the fly.

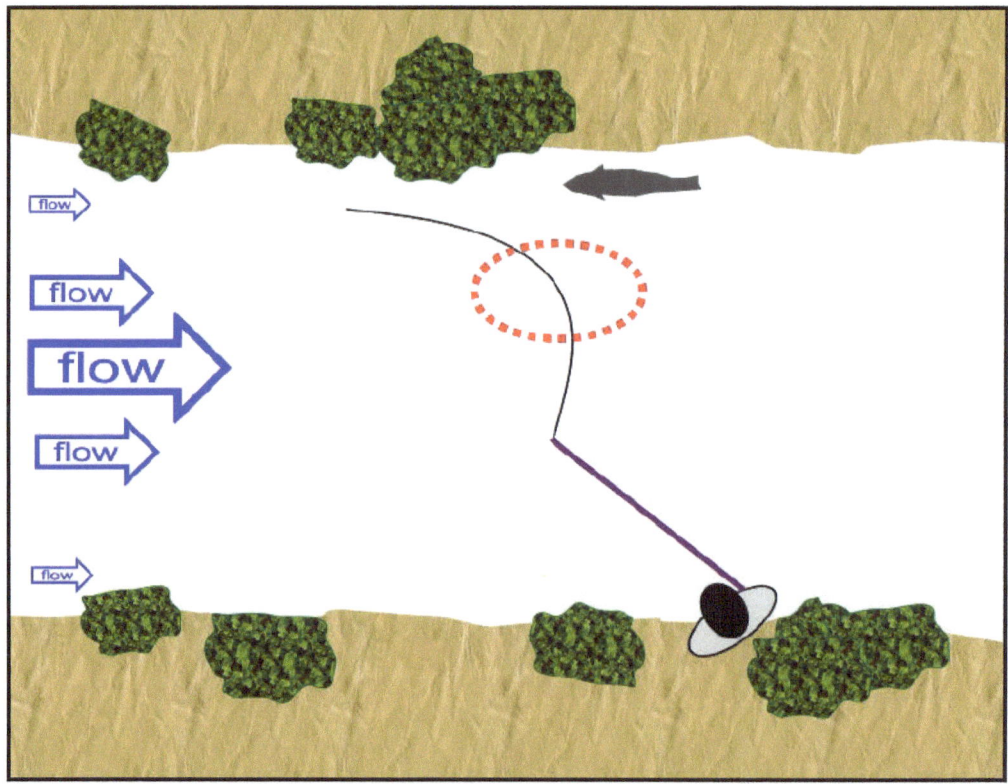

Figure 11 Joe gently lifts just part of the line off the water.

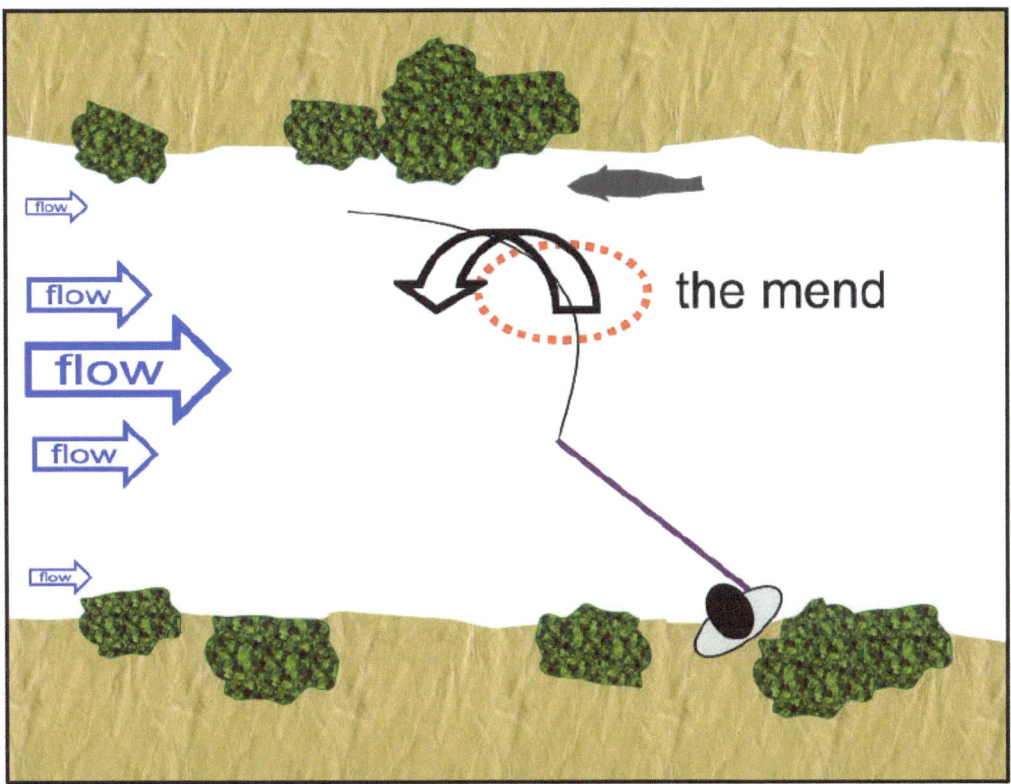

Figure 12 Joe is thinking about what he needs to do. He's going to flip the line upstream just a little bit.

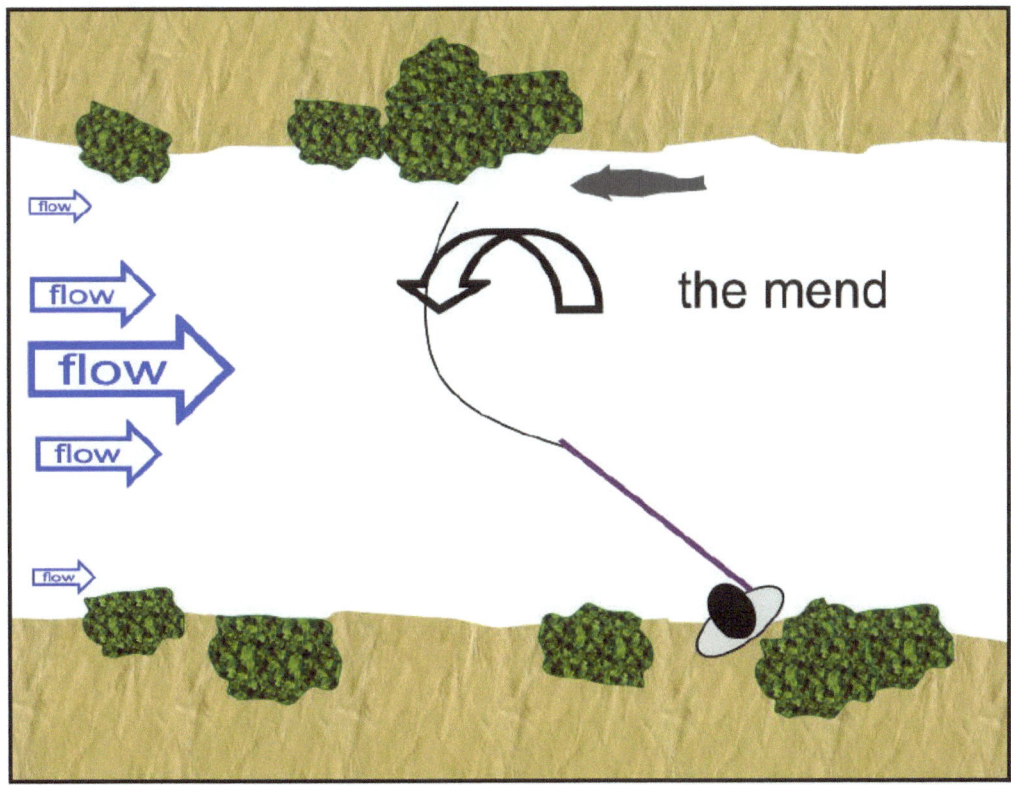

Figure 13 Way to go, Joe! Now the trout will see the fly before it sees the colored part of the line.

HIT THE FAR BANK

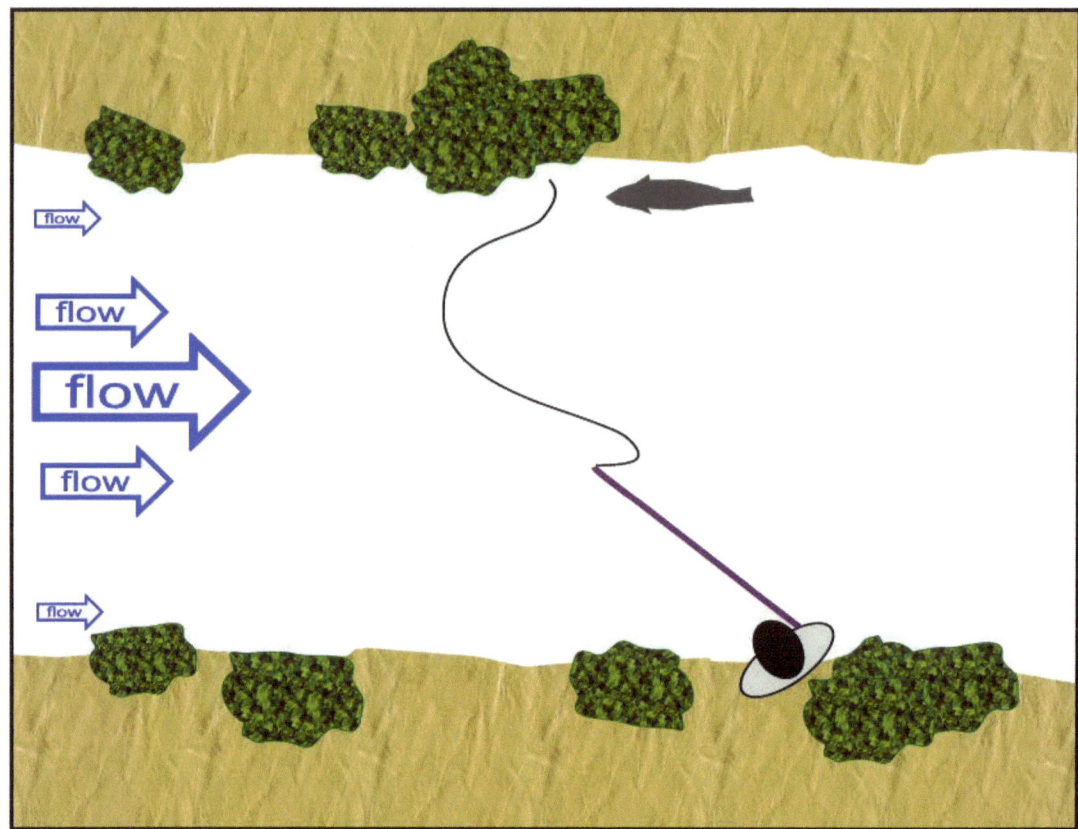

Figure 14 Poor Joe has to keep mending with a lot of mini-mends as the fly slowly drifts down to the trout.

BTW- you can hit specific tricky targets and avoid mending if you give a wiggle to the rod tip at the end of the cast while the line is still in the air, the resultant ziggy-zaggys of line fall on the water. These loops of slacked line will uncoil with the current, flowing downstream faster than the fly but you have time. Your fly will have a moment to rest with a dead drift a few seconds before the unwinding loops eventually sink and yank your fly outta the drift like a bullet. So, you only use this zig-zag method to temporarily hit a specific **target**, like hitting a small foamy eddy on the other side of the fast water. In that case, you want the fly to sit exactly there for at least 10 seconds. Once those loops of slack get pulled tight underwater, that fly is going to ZIP outta there and that action will alert the trout. They will be suspicious of another presentation to the same pocket. You will have to rest that hole and come back later. We only drop ziggy zaggy loops of line on the river to avoid mending when we want to hit very specific small spots on the first and one-time-only cast. Otherwise, Joe Schmo is going to be mending every time he casts. It should simply be a built in instinct. *(Then, you will finally get the many fly fishing jokes based on "Mend! Mend!" and you will be very hip.)*

6. HIGH-STICK THE LINE

Don't let the trout to see the colored part of the fly line before they see the fly. Cast 45^0 upstream to target a fish across from you. Immediately after the fly lands on the water, jump into action because the fly is coming at you and the line is starting to sink in front of the fish!!

1. Point at the fly with the rod tip and follow it as it migrates;
2. Strip line in[11] - pull in the slack line as the fly approaches;

If you have cast your fly 45^0 angle upstream, then the fly is immediately moving downstream toward you and the line is starting to sink and all of this is happening really fast. You have to start quickly picking the line up off the water by stripping it in through your finger on the rod handle (you know that finger?) and letting the gathered line drop at your feet while simultaneously starting to raise your rod tip up in the air to accommodate the approaching fly. (AGH!! KEEP POINTING AT THE FLY!)

---

[11] Stripping means to pull the line with your free hand through the pointing finger of your rod-holding hand. That is, immediately after you cast, lock the line into your first finger against the rod handle and grab the extra line that is hanging down with your free hand. Strip the line through the locked finger and let the excess fall on the water in loops at your feet.

HIGH-STICK THE LINE

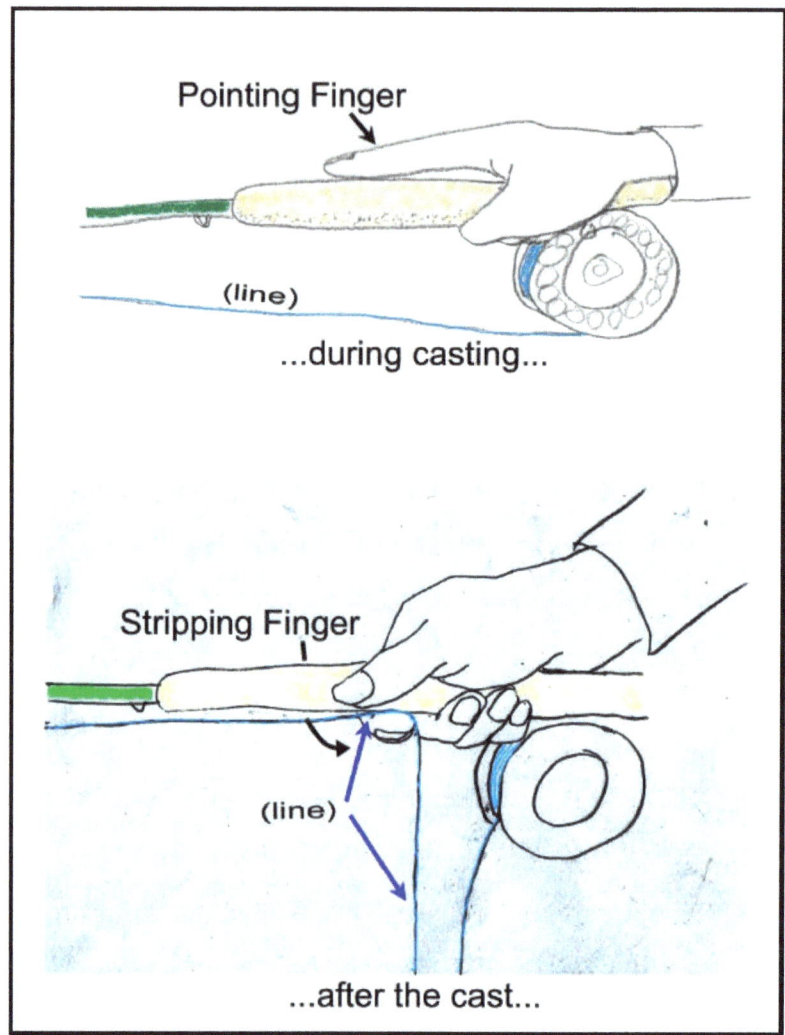

Figure 15 People often use their pointing finger on top of the handle when they are casting for accuracy. After casting, drop your finger below the handle and use your free hand to tuck the line into the stripping finger. The free hand then holds the dangling line and pulls it downward through the stripping finger.

You have to quickly keep lifting more line off the water as the fly comes toward you. Strip and pick up slack line off the water and raise the rod tip at the same rate that the fly is drifting toward you (circus music here because you have to coordinate all of these actions like a circus act...) Strip a little – raise the tip a little – strip a little more – raise the tip a little more – DON'T MEND YET. You've got to match the rate of the drifting fly in order to achieve two things:

1. Drag-free drift (avoid making any suspicious movement of the fly on the surface of the water); and
2. Keep as much line out of the water as you can (this is called high-sticking), so that a wily trout will not see the line before it sees the fly.

When the fly has drifted near enough to you that you can raise the rod and hold the colored part of the line out of the water entirely (only the clear leader is in the water), you are finally "high-sticking" the drifting fly. I like to do this with my arm held as high as I can but with the rod still rather horizontal in the event, I get a strike. If the rod is horizontal, then I still have some upward range in motion available to set the hook. This method of high-sticking works not only for surface fly fishing but also for underwater nymph fishing. Your casting goal is to have the fly slowly drifting near the far bank across from you without any line visible to the trout. As the drift proceeds, gently turn your body to follow the fly as it passes downstream. Eventually, your feet will be pointing downstream.

All of this action as described above is supposed to result in a short cast slightly upstream to the far bank with the fly gently floating drag-free downstream. If you give the cast a little ziggy-zaggy flick before it lands on the water, as described above, then you will have given yourself an advantage over the velocity of the current. You can pick up the line and absorb the loops as the fly comes close enough to high-stick the line.

DON'T LET THE TROUT SEE THE LINE

As the fly meets up with you, hold the rod in the air and high-stick it. As it passes by you, turn and point your feet downstream. Compensate for the "away-game-action" by lowering the rod tip. Point at the fly and start feeding line out fast. You may have to pump the tip of the rod rather viciously to shake more excess line out. (KEEP THE TIP DOWN and POINT AT THE FLY!) You need to give the migrating fly extra line with slack to continue its downstream drift without any drag. Let this rig go way downstream in this manner drifting slowly. Fifty percent of your fishing real estate is downstream of you. Don't underestimate the downstream drift. This is a great change up for a wily trout, which is feeding downstream of a human standing in the water.

In Summary:

- Cast near you
- Lift the line off the water
- Point at the fly

7. THINK LIKE A PUPA

You need to know the underwater insects. You need to know the babies and juveniles of the underwater insects and their behaviors. Let's give you knowledge of pupae. Here:

Pupae live underwater a lot longer than they live as adults in the air or on land. Their time underwater is the longest part of their life (some aquatic insects' lifespan as an adult is so short, they do not even have functional mouths.) The eggs drop from the airborne female adult into the water and fall to the bottom of the stream (or lake). The eggs hatch and the insect begins its life as either a larva (of a future pupa), or a nymph (of a future adult). Larvae are rather primitive animals. Some larvae don't have legs or much of any kind of anatomy other than a body and a mouth. That said, larvae, pupae and nymphs are able to swim somewhat of a bit, though not really propelling themselves with efficiency.

These animals are classified as either plant eaters, detritus eaters, or predators. Some aquatic insects eat algae (bio-film) by scraping the surface of rocks or they munch on detritus (rotten stuff) on the bottom of the streambed between the rocks. Some eat live plants, and some eat each other. For trout to feed on these bugs at this stage of their aquatic life, the trout might snuffle through rocks and pick at the bio-film on the surface of rocks. That is not the most effective way for a trout to feed on an aquatic insect, though. The most opportune situation for a trout is when the insects are (for some reason) suspended in the water column. It is that stage (insects in the water column) that we use our fly patterns and methods to emulate these insects when we fly fish. You will catch more fish if you resolve to utilize this method of presenting an underwater aquatic insect suspended in the water column. We call this method: "nymphing." This means you are going to sink your fly patterns under the surface to emulate a pupa (or nymph or larva…).

Eventually, the larvae will change into a more advanced stage of being an underwater insect. That is, they will morph into a pupa, which, like a nymph is more interesting and capable of doing more things than a larva. The stages of changes in underwater insects' bodies come in cycles. There are "complete" and "incomplete" life cycles for aquatic insects. If you happen to be interested in reciting a lovely bit of scientific prose in the company of other anglers at the bar, then have a try at memorizing this:

- Complete life cycle: egg to larva to pupa to adult (caddis and beetles are like this.)
- Incomplete life cycle: egg to nymph to adult (mayflies and stoneflies are like this.)

An angler needs to know about pupae (and nymphs) in order to select an appropriate fly pattern. Start by observing what insects are in the air at the stream. Did one go zipping by? That was probably not an aquatic insect. A singular bug zipping by your head is probably a terrestrial insect. There happen to be a lot of bugs at streams and lakes that are not aquatic insects. This is why thinking like a pupa is so important. Turning rocks over shows you what kind of insects (what the local pupae and nymphs look like) are in the local water. The behavior of the aquatic insects you see in the air will give you a clue about which pattern to use underwater…

Trout cannot eat insects unless they are in the water. Right? Think about that.

How can you use your observations? No matter how many bugs you see flying around, you should at the least try to discern if they are intermittent unidentified terrestrial bugs, or if they are the same kind hovering in clouds.

If you think you are seeing clouds of mosquitos – are they biting you? Are they silent or buzzing? Midges are tiny flying adult aquatic insects that look like mosquitos. However, mosquitos buzz – midges are silent. Also, midges don't bite – most don't have functional mouths!

If you see clouds of insects hovering above the stream, then you can tell yourself with some confidence, "That is a hatch!" During a hatch event you are only going to catch fish if you emulate one of the stages of the insect's life when it is on the water: that is, emerging or failed or drowning adult insects. If you consider the behavior of pupae (and nymphs) during a hatch, then you can fish all the stages of the aquatic insects that are available to a trout that lead up to and include the hatch event.

Ninety percent of the time, trout are feeding on the underwater stage of an aquatic insects' life. Everyone who fly fishes should know this. Trust me. Or, ask Brian Heinold, with Colorado Parks and Wildlife Aquatic Research Division, Professor of Entomology at Colorado Mountain College, Leadville, Colorado in the Professional Fly Fishing Guide certification program. My mentor of 20+ years – Doug, whom I married - was the first person to tell me this fact, which he learned from his mentor, Kim Keeley – one of Idaho's preeminent woman fly fishing guides some thirty years ago. I'll have to ask Kim where she learned this fact about 99% of a trout's diet being the underwater stage of an aquatic insect's life. Perhaps Kim learned from the Coeur d'Alene, Nez Perce or Kootenai people of Idaho who have been studying trout behavior for 30,000 years? Let it be known, Joe Schmo, trout are eating underwater insects most of the time.

Female adult aquatic insects drop their eggs into the water and the nearly microscopic eggs sink down to the rocks. The eggs will produce either a primitive larva or a nymph (depending on whether or not the species has a complete or incomplete life cycle). The larvae and nymphs live on and in between the rocks on the bottom of the stream. We don't usually try to emulate larvae and nymphs living in rocks because that is a difficult horizon of the stream to work. We usually try to emulate pupae or nymphs freely floating in the water column.

Pupae (not nymphs) happen to be a bit more physiologically advanced than a larva. Pupae never eat!! They stay in one place until they swim to the surface to become adults. They are very actively developing adult body parts by "rearranging" their juvenile body parts as they age. Mature pupae are enclosed in a sheath, like a tamale. They have the adult mouthparts, antennae, legs, and wings just about fully formed while still living underwater. An artificial "nymph" pattern with sprouting wings, a tail, and herl (peacock feather fuzz) around the head of the pattern to emulate gills or little legs would resemble this stage well. Patterns like Bead-head Pheasant Tail, Hare's Ear or some kind of callibaetis pattern would work well for this stage. These patterns enhance parts that look like thorax, legs, gills, tail and wings sacks.

Aquatic Insect Mobility

Pupae are sessile while developing their adult body parts. They stay in one place living in the rocks, in colonies of the same species. Nymphs will actively move around looking for food. Trout snuffle for both the sessile pupae and the scurrying nymphs. Under occasional circumstances due to the fluctuations in a stream's flow or some catastrophe, pupae and nymphs can get swept into the current. (Sometimes, a pupa or nymph may leap into the current to catch a short ride downstream.) Usually, though, these animals are living the life for an aquatic insect totally underwater in the rocks with all their friends and they are not going anywhere. This is the main stage of their life: underwater eaters.

Despite how happy a pupa (or nymph) can be, there will come a day when its body is going to start changing and they're never going to come back. Many species cut their way out of their husk while still living underwater and the adult swims to the surface. Some species climb out onto rocks to shed their outer sheath and then they climb or fly to bushes. Some pupae may collect oxygen around their external bodies with tiny hairs and eventually become buoyant. Some species of pupae begin to absorb oxygen directly out of the water and store this growing bubble in an area proximal to their wing sack. There is a fully formed adult inside its shuck. Many pupae, such as the type that absorbs oxygen, will have a lump or bump where the wing sack will grow. We tie fly patterns that emulate this bulging wing sack. When the oxygen bubble starts to form, the wing bulge becomes iridescent. There are some mayfly pupae whose external wing cases turn really dark as the inner wing pulls away from the exoskeleton. That is why we have both dark and iridescent "flashback" pupae fly patterns.

Buoyant pupae are at the mercy of the current as they float up to the surface of the water. This is a very crucial stage for the pupae (and trout). They are completely vulnerable in this suspended state. The trapped air gives them an iridescent sheen. They cannot swim or propel with any efficiency. They may be screaming with terror, these buoyant pupae - we can only speculate.

Pupae or nymphs that become dislodged, or adults that are swimming to the surface, or pupae that are buoyant are a trout's main meal because they are suspended in the water column. The haphazard insects are simply tumbling with the current and have no means of propelling themselves out of harm's way (though some species are fairly feeble swimmers). This is a great opportunity for a feeding trout. These drifting insects are the triggers the trout are keying in on when facing upstream. (Free-floating buoyant pupae species and ascending adults are great patterns for fly fishers to utilize.) Due to the vulnerability of an insect in this state, an emergence event will launch thousands of thousands of swimming and emerging adults all at the same time in order to engulf the habitat and create a barrage of rising insects so that by vast numbers some of the ascending animals actually make it to the surface. We call this a hatch, though more specifically, it is an event where the adult is emerging from its pupa or nymph stage.

THE HATCH

"A hatch should mean a lot more than a dry fly to an angler. It should mean an emergence pattern or drowned adult or spinner, as well." – (Raupp, 2019) – "The Bug Guy"

The physical parameters that trigger an emergence event are time, temperature, and pressure[12]

- Time: the season as perceived by the length of daylight;
- Water Temperature: driven by climate, weather and cloud over; and
- Pressure: either barometric pressure dropping or rising, or isostatic pressure as the water depth changes.

---

[12]The effects of pressure on pupae behavior is my personal conjecture based on personal observation. Dropping barometric pressure has been observed to produce a positive outcome for fishing, which I attribute to the activity of emerging pupae not just happy trout; Dropping barometric pressure produces cloud cover, which effects lighting as a factor in fish feeding, but I also think the diffuse light triggers the activity of the pupae; Also, the isostatic pressure from water depth exerted on a pupa is relieved as it ascends. I am speculating that the influence of barometric and isostatic pressure is significant on the physiological nature of these tiny creatures because their size makes them more susceptible to minute fluctuations in their habitat. Go ahead -change my mind.

(The element of pressure is my personal opinion based on observation. There are no studies that I know of to test the effects of varying pressure on aquatic species emergence in support my hypothesis, but as a geologist I base this speculation on understanding how chemical reactions occur in a natural environment under the same effects of time, temperature and pressure. Also, generations of grizzled old anglers are a source for myriads of fishing lore and rules based on tidal or moon phases, and barometric pressure related to incoming or outgoing weather.)

During the emergence event of some species, inside the pupae husk there is a fully developed adult stuffed like a tamale. In some cases, the adult cuts open the casing and swims to the surface. In other cases, dependent on species, either the nymph or the pupa ascends due to buoyancy. The isostatic pressure on its body diminishes with shallowing depth. Also, the light increases as the animal rises in the water column. These perceived changes cause the adult to squirm inside the husk. This little animal will intermittently twitch as it ascends. (That is an action the angler can add to the drift of a nymph pattern – give it a little jigging action.) The insect is agitated. When (if) it reaches the surface, the husks split open. If there is a buoyant wing sack, that sack will immediately dry and crack open. In any case, the bunched up wings expel coming out in a loop before extending straight up; the adult pulls itself out of the husk and steps out onto the water and the wings stiffen up. Then, it flies away. All of this action from ascent to flying away occurs in less than a minute. I've observed this!

At any moment in the "hatch" event, any of the stages of emergence can fail. The wing sack can bust open underwater causing the creature to drown. An adult cutting its way out of its sheath can fail and drown. The wings can get stuck to the surface of the water. Though, a fully formed emerging adult has water-repelling (hydrophobic) hairs on its wings that help it keep from sticking to the surface, the wings may still get swamped. In that case, the adult will drown and die. After the successful adult flies off, the hydrophobic hairs fall off the wings. (The result is rather dull-looking wings with crisp edges on adults at the beginning of a hatch but brilliantly white ratty wings on the adult at the end of the day.) If an adult accidentally sticks to the water, its wings are often laid to one side. We use CDC ("cul de canard" - oily duck butt) feathers tied into "loop-wing" style emerging fly patterns to emulate these swamped hair-covered wings. CDC floats a long time before it becomes saturated. When a flying adult weakens and fails (its life is spent) it falls with splayed wings on the water. We call this condition a spent "spinner" pattern. The artificial fly pattern for a spent sinner would utilize bright white fuzzy rayon material for the wings to emulate the ratty white wings.

TROUT ARE FEEDING ON THE EMERGING INSECTS AT ALL STAGES DURING THE ENTIRE HATCH EVENT

THINK LIKE A PUPA

There is a phenomenon that happens at the head of a riffles section. Immediately upstream of the riffle, which is a shallow zone, the stream is deeper. As the stream bed shallows out, the larger volume of water stacks up. The slowing water bunches the emerging pupae / nymphs / adults together and pushes them upward. The degree of light they are exposed to increases as they rise. The isostatic pressure drops due to shallowing depth. The result is a concentration of newly emerged adults hovering in a cloud at the head of a riffles section. All of the failed adults are drifting downstream either on the surface or sinking just below the surface – drowned emerging pupae, nymphs, drowned adults, etc. are tumbling in the water column. Trout in the riffles are slurping up the unsuccessful insects. Good fly patterns to use during a hatch in a riffles section would be foam-post emergers, loop-wing emergers, CDC emergers, WD40s, flashback patterns, spinners, and the such.

UNDERSTANDING PUPAE BEHAVIOR IS WHY WE FISH RIFFLES DURING A HATCH

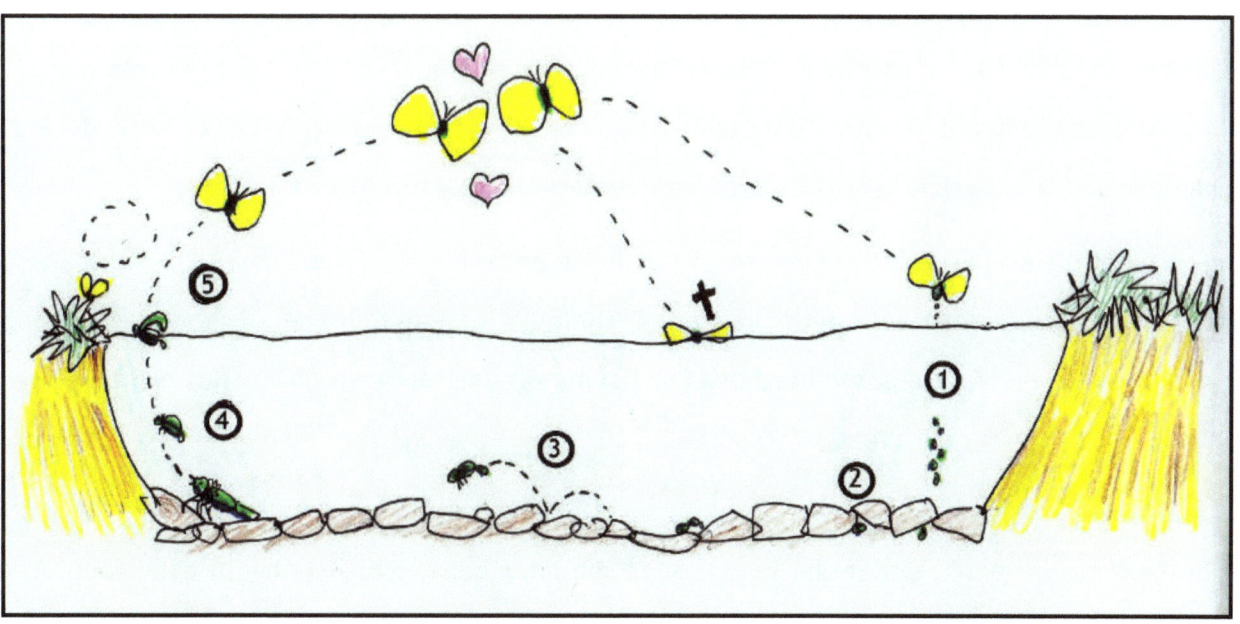

Figure 16 Common life cycle of an aquatic insect (idealized). 1) eggs fall from adult female through the water column to the bottom; 2) larvae live in the rocks; 3) developing pupae/larvae/nymphs happily living underwater; 4) emerging event pupae-to-adult; 5) mustering adults, mating and dying.

8. FACE DOWNSTREAM

When your fly drifts past you, turn and face downstream, which, for your edification is considered to be backwards. It's inside out. Some people think this method is just plain wrong. Passer-byers will smirk at you as if they are more knowledgeable about this sport. They don't realize you know exactly what you are doing. There is method to your madness. You are thinking creatively and tricking a picky trout in a technical water by using an unorthodox fishing technique. Good for you. The educated trout are not expecting this behavior from a typical fly fishing human. You're gonna win.

The point of all this high-sticking and keeping the line off the water is because you do not want the trout to see the colored part of the line before it sees the fly. This is technical water. It's a tailwater. Lots of people fish here every day, day-in and day-out all year round. The trout remember experiences and they know that if they see a line, there is a fly attached to a fisherman. They're not going to flee because there is nowhere to go. They will hunker down and let the line pass over their head. If you are really messy, they might actually duck under the line and use their snout to push it over. This is the behavior of a tricky trout in a tailwater.

Depending on what the stream looks like where you chose to enter the water and cast to the far bank, you now have to play the water downstream with different techniques that match the situation depending on the character of the water. Here are some methods for fishing downstream on either flat calm water or riffley bumpy water:

FLAT CALM CLEAR WATER

Keep the fly next to the bank, either the far bank or the near bank, whichever you can reach. In order to accomplish this, you might have to gently flip some mends of the colored line toward the bank from where you are and then tighten the line in order to "feed" that mend in the line downstream and nurse that kink in the line to propagate downstream. When the kink reaches the fly, it will drag the fly over to the bank in the direction you have tossed the mend. This is a great way to get flies to migrate under low overhanging bushes rather than trying to cast under the bush. Cast upstream of the bush and flip some mends against the bank then let the mend propagate downstream until it pulls the fly under the bush.

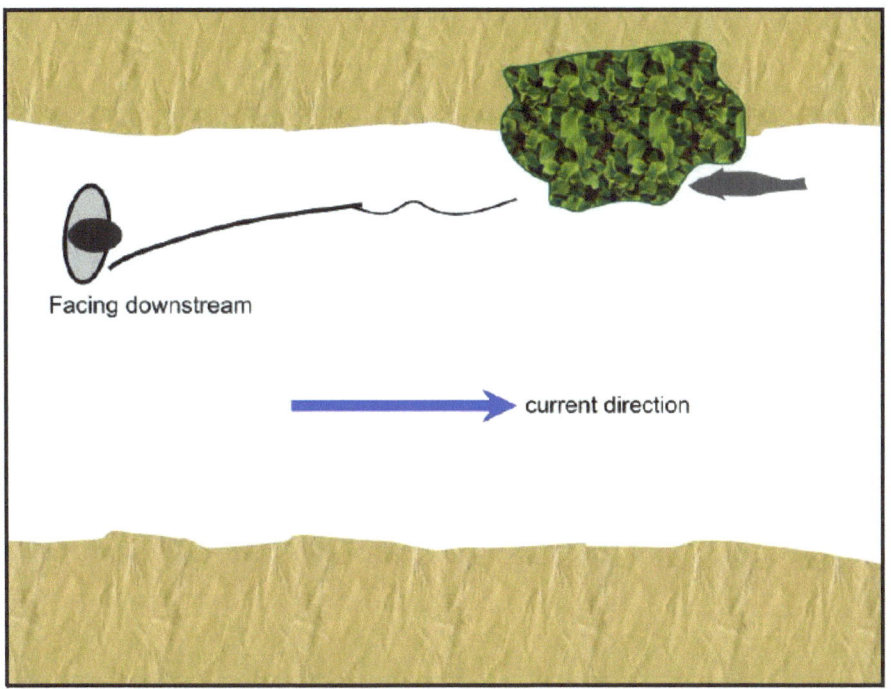

Figure 17 Facing downstream, the fly might tend to migrate away from the bank.

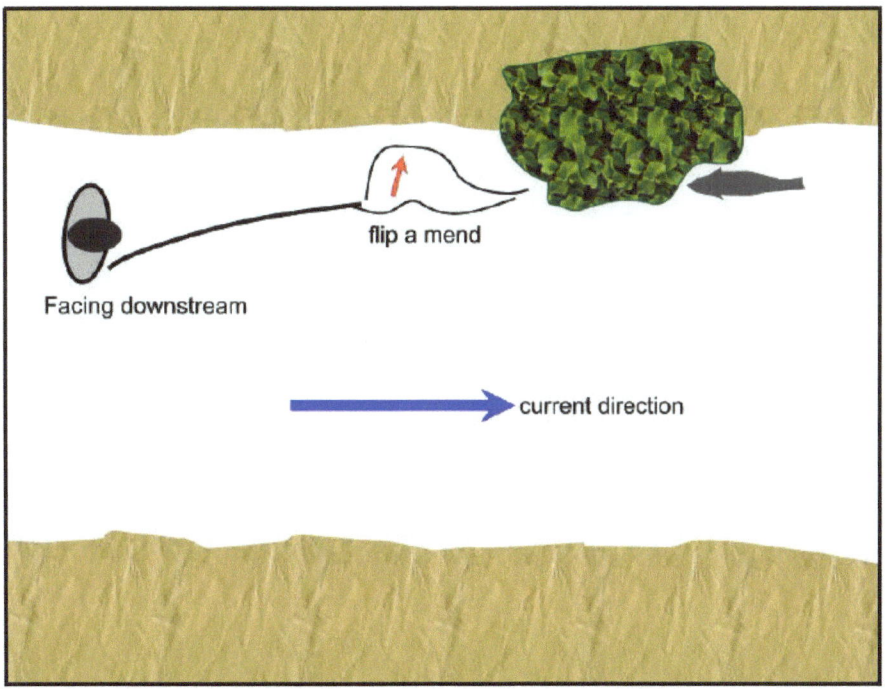

Figure 18 Flip a mend against the bank and tighten the line.

FACE DOWNSTREAM

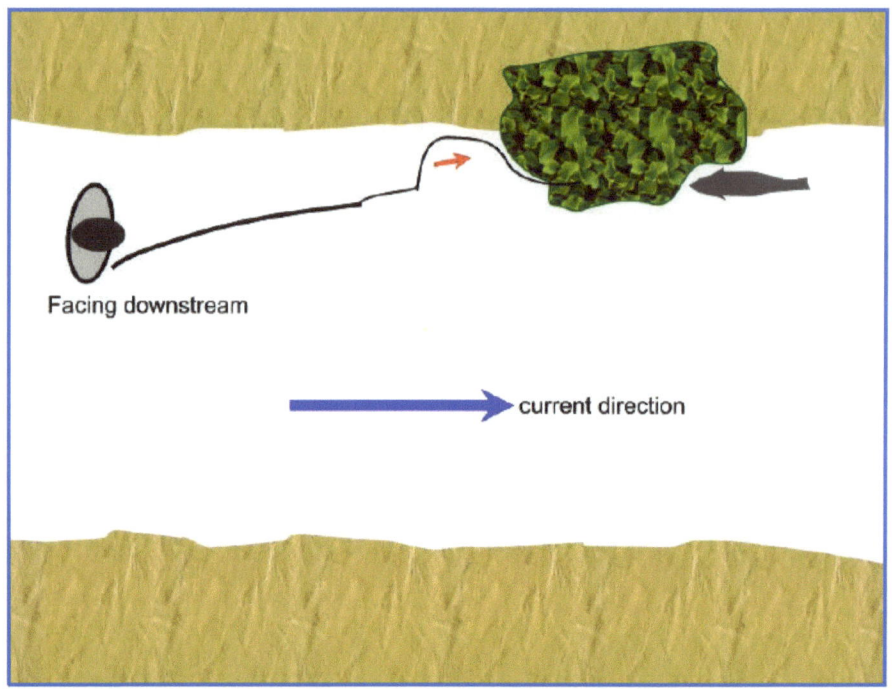

Figure 19 Keep the line tight so the mend will propagate downstream.

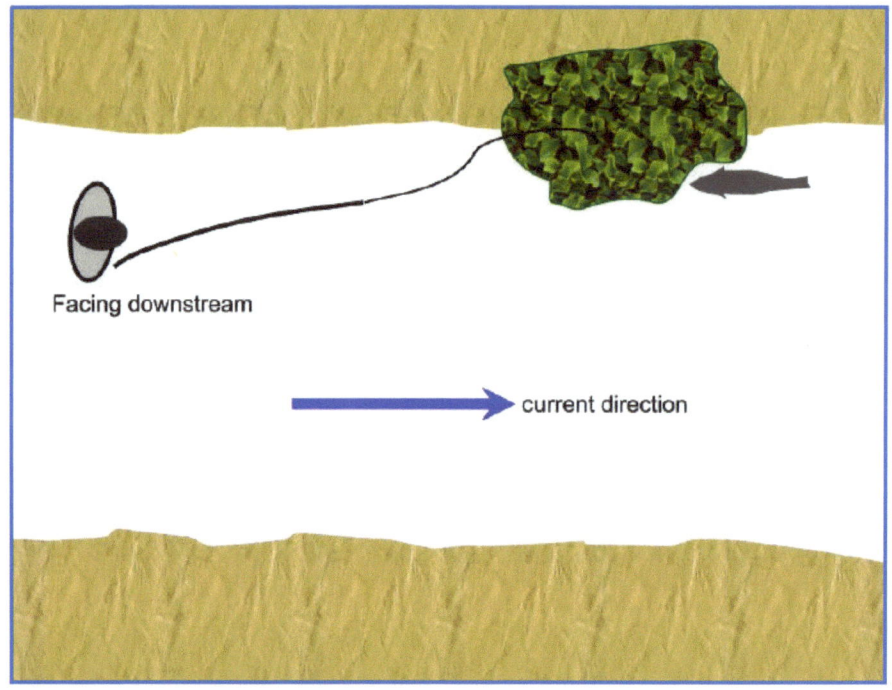

Figure 20 The mend will catch up with the fly and pull in the direction of the mend. In this case, the mend will pull the fly under the bush.

SKATING OVER RIFFLES

When the water is flat and calm (like a mirror), you and other predators can see the trout, like this:

Figure 21 here lies a vulnerable trout. Do you see it, Joe?

When the water flows fast over a shallow zone with a cobbly (rocky) bottom, the riffles (bumps) obscure the trout. No one can see the trout. It likes to hide under riffles for this reason.

Figure 22 sneaky trout…. Though, I can still see it, Joe.

It's OK if you cannot see the trout. Have faith. It's there. They have nowhere to go and they are likely just waiting for you to leave. Plus, most people fish facing upstream. No one fishes downstream. That's backwards. So, wily trout are more at ease downstream of you. They have memory and in their experience: they are safe when they move downstream of you.

The trout in the riffles is nestled between large cobbles that are deflecting the powerful current around them. They are in a "pressure shadow" behind large cobbles or boulders. Trout hold in low-profile holes where the bottom of the stream has been scoured out. They are hanging out underneath the bulk of the fast current streaming overhead. They are watching. Their amazing eyes are clueing in on the debris that is coming at them. They have about 8 feet vision directly in front of them to decide whether or not the approaching speck is a pupa / nymph or a leaf particle. They are not going to invest much more energy than a slight twist to the side and back again. They don't want to get pushed out of their nice hiding place: conservation of energy wins in the animal kingdom.

> *NOTE: The margin between a fast part of the water and a slow part of the water makes a 3-dimensional plane from the surface all the way through the water to the bottom of the stream. That change between fast and slow water is a friction zone that catches debris and drifting insects and spins them in place. The trout set up in the slow water and pick the specks of food out of this plane as if they are looking at a flat screen TV. Put your pattern inside the slow water and let it get caught up in that plane of friction. BOOM!*

A trout will leave its lair (pop up to the surface or bend its whole body into the current) to follow a big button of food that is nutritious enough to warrant spending energy. A trout will chase a hopper pattern or a streamer because those patterns emulate large insects or animals that provide a large portion of nutrition to warrant the expenditure of that much energy.

> *NOTE: Every year, our local Pikes Peak Chapter of Trout Unlimited invites the renowned fly fishing expert, Landon Mayer, to speak at one of our membership meetings. Landon shows a video he recorded of hooking into a large brown trout when all of the sudden, a much larger gigantic brown trout enters the scene and then disappears back into the hold. Landon lands the larger trout first and he keeps a second rod pre-rigged for gigantic monsters. After he landed the one, he immediately went for the bigger one.*
> *(Mayer, 2019)*

Point being, trout (and all wildlife) have a quota of energy to amass without spending too much energy – an equilibrium of expenditure. Trout will compete for feeding on large morsels. Not so with a mayfly. Nor a pupa. Nor a small midge. Those morsels are too small to make a fish chase it in fast water (normally).

> *"A trout has to be reasonable about the amount of energy it invests in catching its dinner."*

Trout in the riffles are basically feeding on tiny pupae and nymphs as the insects tumble adrift in the water column. Sometimes, trout feed on an opportunistic treat like a worm or drowned terrestrial that is floating by. All they have to do is deflect their tail into the current to divert their head to the side and suck the passing insect into their mouth. Then, they return to their station, facing upstream lining up on the next snack in the water column. They do this about 90% of their time. (The other 10% of their life is literally resting...ZZZzzzzzzzz...)

FISH SLEEP. THEY ALSO YAWN.

9. TUMBLE DRY FLIES UNDERWATER

DROWNED TERRESTRIALS

The other means by which trout are feeding in riffles is they sidle downstream to pick up a submerged (drowned) terrestrial, like an ant or a hopper, that they see tumbling in the current. These unfortunate insects hit the water hard, wiggle a bit, then drown and sink. Trout see them hit the water. They see them wiggle. They see them sink. If the terrestrial is at all suspicious-looking, a wily trout will not only ignore it, it may actually leave the riffles and move away because it is alarmed by your rubber and plastic hopper. Since riffles are shallow, a trout feels vulnerable when it is discovered because it doesn't have much depth to hide in. (There is one ridiculous exception to this rule: The rubber-legged Purple Chubby. Everyone loves a chubby, especially a trout in a riffle. They feel ridiculous though, when they take one…)

> *"A trout feels vulnerable in shallow water."*

As a consequence, you may not have a good result when using a rubber-legged terrestrial pattern in technical water because the wily trout is suspicious of it. HOWEVER - if you let it sink and go tumbling down the tongue[13] of the stream over an edge into a deep pool, you might pick up a big trout. The tongue of the chute of water is fast and powerful. The pool at the bottom of a chute's tongue is turbid with elevated oxygen levels and swirling debris, which includes drowned insects. Big trout hang out in these deep pools and they feed on larger snacks, especially in summer when the rest of the river may be getting uncomfortably warm.

If you are facing downstream and the water drops down a tongue into a deep hole, feed your line out and send a terrestrial pattern overboard. Let the fly tumble underwater in the current. Hold the rod over the edge and allow the fly to drift around in the pool without any action. Don't jig it. Drowned insects do not swim. They drift and tumble. You can pick up a large fish this way but then you must guide them downstream to a shallow place to land them. Plan ahead – if you don't have enough real estate to land a large fish downstream then don't hook them. You cannot pull a large trout up a tongue out of a hole.

> *Think about your plan to land the fish and make a decision prior to hooking into one.*

---

[13] A "tongue" is what I call kayaking-type of big water where the stream is choked through a narrow margin between boulders and drops down into a deep hole at the end of the chute – the upper flat part of the water as it drops over the edge is a "tongue".

PART B: SOME DETAILS

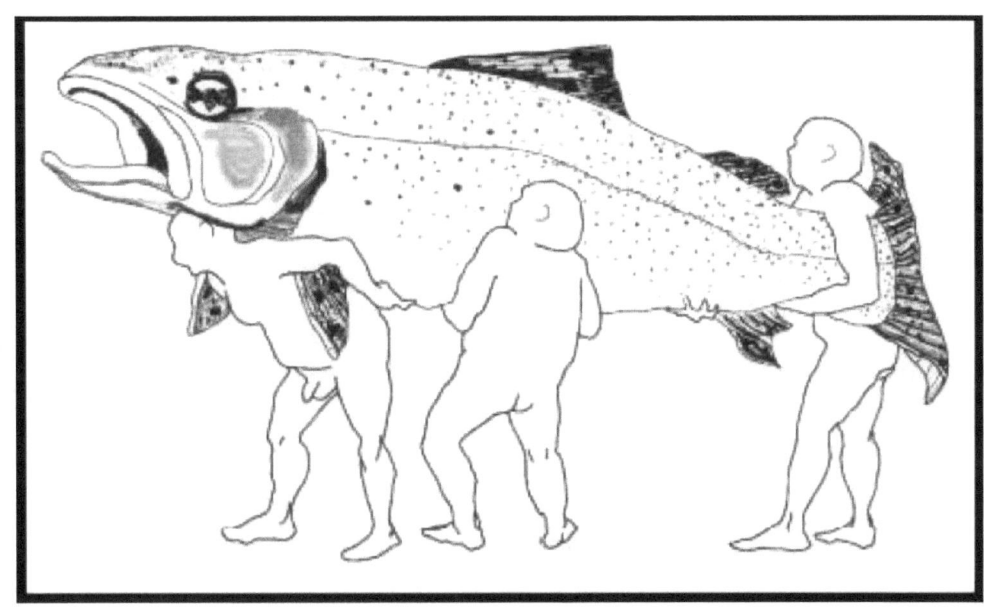

45

1. NYMPHING ALL THE WATER

Nymphing the Entire Water Column

For nymphing, you are going to have to first decide if you need to drift your flies vertical to each other, such as through a deep slow hole, or horizontal to each other in shallower fast runs. This choice depends on the depth and velocity of the water and / or arrangement of the feeding fish (if you can see them). You have to look at the water and decide your plan of attack. Then, rig your nymphing set up according to your mentally superior plan.

Nymphing Deep Pools

If you suspect there might be big trout hanging out in a deep pool, rig your flies so they drift vertical to each other. This is because trout in deep pools have a lot of vertical room to rise and sink without coming to the surface. They maybe be feeding in a specific stratigraphic horizon, as well. You need to figure out how deep or how shallow they are feeding by changing where you put your strike indicator. (Slide the strike indicator up or down to put the flies in the trout's feeding horizon.) Their preferred feeding horizon may be the result of a specific stage of pupae development as listed above, where pupae are susceptible to changes in pressure, temperature and light, all of which trigger a pupa to begin a stage of emergence. Remember? A pre-emergent pupa absorbs oxygen and becomes buoyant? That is why a deep hole (or a lake) requires figuring out the horizon at which the trout are feeding, i.e. the horizon the pupae are likely to be suspended. To control the flies to drift in vertical array, put the split shot at the very end of the leader instead of above the point fly and use a "tag"[14] to attach dropper flies. *WHAT?* TAGS?? Here – look:

---

[14] See Section 4 – Rigging for Streams…

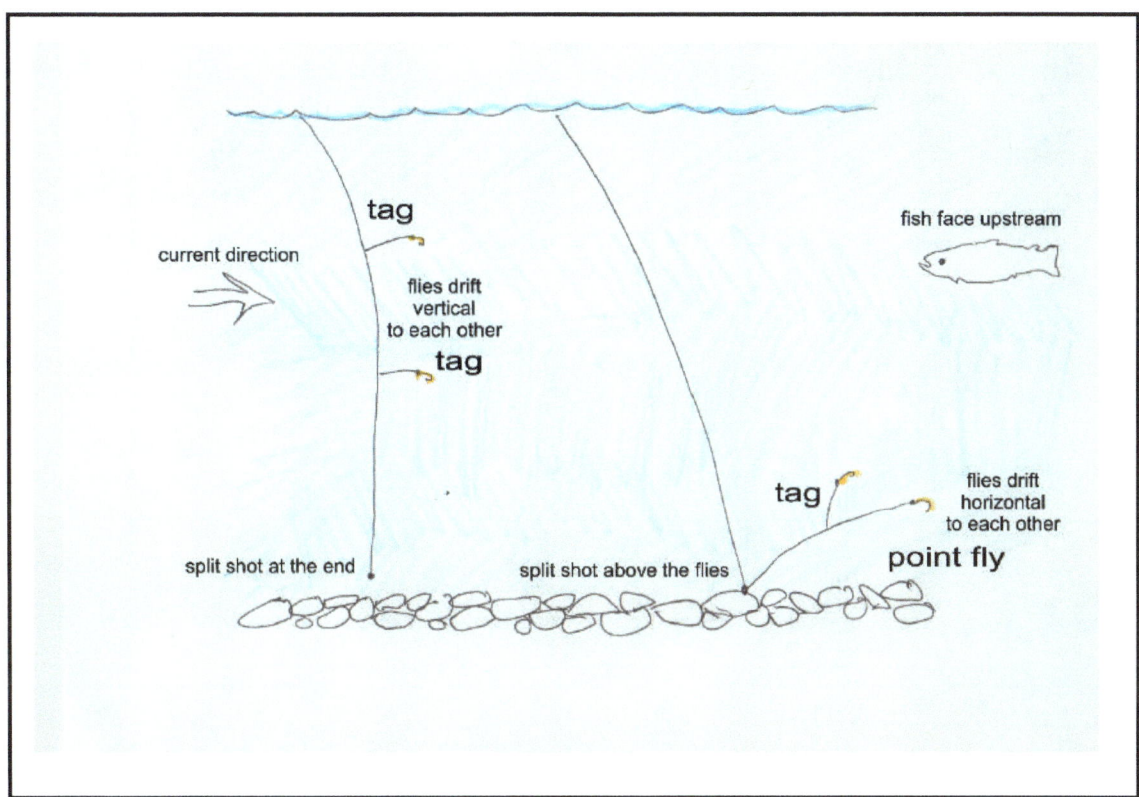

Figure 23 How the tags stick-out and how split shot works either above or below the fly patterns.

NYMPHING SHALLOW WATER

At places where there are riffles and runs[15], the trout are likely hanging out in a dispersed pod. They are rather spread out to cover the stream from margin to margin even if some trout are hanging a bit further upstream than others. The trout are nestled between cobbles in a horizontal array with their buddies. They are feeding together on anything that is tumbling downstream to them.

You can create a horizontal array (more or less) of your flies by putting the split shot above the flies. The closer the split shot is to the flies, the lower the flies will ride in the water column. If the shot is too close (within a foot) the trout might reject the flies. Light flies, (like small #20 or #22 simple zebra midge nymph patterns) will ride higher in the water column. Heavier flies, (#14 or #16 with beads, wire, or complex body parts like rubber legs) will ride lower in the water column. You can keep your flies down using split shot and also maybe add a heavy tungsten beaded nymph as a point fly.

---

[15] Riffles: Fast water flowing in a shallow zone over underwater cobbles producing a bumpy surface or Runs: main body of water flowing through a straight channel where the surface is rather smooth.

Figure 24 Split shot above the flies presents them in a more-or-less horizontal array but the current will still move the flies around. Lighter flies ride higher than heavy flies.

2. SKATING AND SWINGING

There are some species of adult insects (both aquatic and terrestrial) that hit the water hard and either twitch or scurry across the surface before they ultimately drown. Grasshoppers, beetles, and ants are famous twitchers. Caddis, stoneflies, damsel flies commonly scurry across the surface. Assess the character of the water. If the water is flowing fast but is riffley (bumpy), the trout are probably hanging out in between cobbles and looking upward. These trout can be triggered when an insect plops onto the surface and subsequently scurries across the water. If you mimic this action on the surface with a bushy fly, like a caddis or big (#14+) Parachute Adams with a prominent white post, the trout will often make a fast hit without even thinking. The trout don't have enough time to investigate thoroughly in this fast shallow water. So, they often hit the fly hard in response to this plop and scurry action (the way YOU made it move: the fly's action – your growing skill and finesse).b

One of the most productive actions in your unorthodox fishing methodology for catching wily trout in a technical water, is to let your flies swing across the current after it has drifted downstream from you – nymph patterns or dry flies -- meaning you can swing the fly patterns whether you are fishing underwater or on the surface. This action isn't so straightforward because you don't want to scare the fish with a "motorboat" style of drag. You need to tantalize them. There is a degree of finesse to a nice, taunting swing depending on the fly pattern. I break this methodology into two ideas: swinging nymphs and / or skating a dry fly.

SWINGING A NYMPH PATTERN

Swinging a nymph means letting the submerged pattern swing up to the surface. Since aquatic insects are not propelling themselves underwater, the rate at which you swing a nymphing fly needs to be slow. The rate of the swing should ideally match the natural ascent of an emerging adult. To control this swing, let the fly line spool out as the fly drifts downstream. Keep pointing the rod tip at the fly (where you think your fly is, because in riffley water you may not be able to see it) with the tip down and wiggle the line out. When the line and fly are a good way downstream, tuck the line into your stripping finger[16] and hold it taut. Let your nymphing rig waggle underwater downstream a moment with your rod tip lowered. When you stopped letting line out by trapping the line with your stripping finger, the nymph pattern(s) swung up to the surface. Now, they are waggling in the

---

[16] Stripping finger – the pointing finger on the hand that is grasping the handle of the rod. Hold the line with this trigger finger.

water near the surface. This is an effective method for taunting trout in riffles. Get ready for a hit before you gently lift for the next cast.

To understand what a trout is doing when you swing a nymph fly, review the trout's behavior:

A trout in fast shallow water is keeping a low profile behind rocks or hanging out under the main current. The trout is watching upstream for a target to eat. Hapless nymphs or pupae are tumbling in the current downstream toward the trout. A trout is focusing on specks in the water about 8 feet upstream from their lair. The trout will start to line up on an insect when it is within about 4-5 feet. The trout will conserve energy by simply tilting its pectoral fins to lift its head up to take the insect (fly) and then sink back to its hole. Or, it will use its tail to bend into the current and pick the fly up, then return to its holding place, gently turning in a loop. When you let your line out and send a nymph fly downstream and then let it lift up to the surface, a trout will key in on that movement and pick up that specific fly with intent to return to its lair. When the trout turns from its "take" to return to its lair, the hook will set.

If you don't get a hit right away, get ready to change your cast. Before you cast and while your rig is still undulating in the water downstream of you, slowly lift the rod tip and also strip some of the line in to load the rod before you cast. The downstream pull of the current will help load the rod for the next cast. To re-cast, lift all the stuff you have rigged (strike indicator, weight, point fly and dropper) slowly up with one motion and when it comes free of the water, point the rod upstream to a place you have targeted – all in one fell swoop. No false cast. A good practice would be to look upstream before you lift and load the rod. Don't pluck the rig out of the water with verve or it will make a suspicious popping sound. Lift and plop upstream with conservation and try to time for that exact moment when the underwater gear comes clear of the water and is flying airborne. If you pick a place upstream with your eye before you lift the gear out of the water, then you can land a cast in one motion without having to false cast in the air and thereby limit how much action you are subjecting the trout to. Remember – conservation of action keeps the trout from becoming wary of you. Try to obtain one smooth motion to pull the rig out of the water and fling it to a desired target upstream. I often get a hit when I am looking upstream for my next cast. The trout hit my nymph as it is waggling downstream of me. This may be due to emulating the rise of an emerging adult insect.

> *NOTE: Because trout are hanging out in a lair lining up on a target drifting down to them, you wouldn't know if you just pulled the whole rig up and out of their lineup just as they were about to take the fly. That is why when nymphing, we cast in the same run over and over.*

SKATING AND SWINGING

Skating a Dry Fly Pattern

If you are casting a dry fly rig (1 or 2 flies) across the current or upstream in a riffle section, you must <u>mend immediately</u> and then high stick the line up in the air as the fly passes you by in order to keep the colored part of the line upstream of the fly. (You want the trout to see the fly before they see the line). After the fly has drifted downstream of your position, turn your feet to follow the fly downstream. Feed some of the line out by holding the rod tip down and wiggling the tip. It's OK to let the fly start to skate across the surface. The dry fly will start to swing across the current on top of the water until it arrives exactly downstream of your position. Trap the line with your stripping finger and hold the line tight to keep the fly on the surface of the water. Let it dance or skate around on the surface of the water. Ideally, if you hold the rod up in the air a bit you can start skating the fly from the far bank (not too fast) toward the center of the stream letting it bob up and down over the riffles. You want the pattern riding on the surface naturally without making a big "V"-shaped drag.[17] When you are skating a fly on the surface, the trout often flip over the fly with a sudden splash and may even come partially out of the water. This aggressive take is usually easy to see but unfortunately, it is so unexpected that the angler often doesn't react in time to set the hook. There will be an explosive flop in the water at the fly and then a *bang-bang-bang* on the end of the line -- SET!!! By "set" I mean gently but swiftly pull the rod tip to the side – not up. Sweep to the side when setting the hook on a fish that is downstream.

Setting a hook on a downstream trout has the tricky liability of pulling the hook out of its open mouth. If you side-swipe the rod tip, you can twist the hook in its mouth. Then, nurse the trout over to the near bank. Don't horse a downstream trout. It has the current in its favor and you run the risk of it throwing the hook or breaking the fly off if you horse the fish. Raise your rod tip and keep enough tension to allow the rod to follow the bucking fish but not too much tension or the trout will break off. Walk into the fish (follow it downstream and reel the line in). Let the fish be a fish. Let it go where it wants to go but don't let it get its head down. You walk closer to the downstream fish, rather than pulling a fish up to you.

---

[17] If the fly is sitting too low in the water, it will make a "V"-shaped wake behind it. Either use a lighter fly, a smaller fly, or hold the line higher over the water to avoid this effect.

3. SETTING THE HOOK AND LANDING A BIG FISH

SEEING THE TAKE

A lot of big fish got to be so big because they became wily. Their "takes" are commonly subtle. There are different tell-tell signs to look for when a fish takes your fly. It's not always so obvious. In general, if you see any kind of swirl or dent in the vicinity of where you think your fly is (remember – you are constantly pointing your rod tip at the fly on the water as it moves downstream, right?), go ahead and assume something took your fly – set the hook! Basically, if you see something on the surface, that odd disturbance might be a fish taking your fly. It's worth the experiment to set the hook.

Most of the time, you will see rings on the water made by trout sticking their noses out of the water with open mouths when they are consistently feeding. If you watch these rings you will begin to see the trout's nose, not just a ring on the water. You are developing your "wildlife eyes". That is, you are learning to see the trace of an animal against the backdrop of its habitat.

The usual mode of surface feeding for a wild trout in a wild stream is to breach the water with its nose and open mouth, then close its mouth over the insect. Then, submerge. You can actually see their mouths open and then close at the surface. However, the more timid, careful trout will commonly rise to just under the surface and inspect the fly closely. This wily trout is looking for the tippet, for the leader, for the fly line. It's looking for YOU on the bank! Hopefully, the trout will then open its mouth and suck the fly down from under the surface. This action also leaves a telltale ring on the water or sometimes it is only a pucker. You don't actually see the trout snout. Just a ring on the water. If you see a trout's back or dorsal fin, it is possibly investigating the fly out of suspicion rather than taking it in its mouth. There are videos of tailwater-dwelling trout rising to a fly, shouldering it, and spinning around to look at it closely to see if it is a natural or an artificial. If you see a trout's tail, this fish has just rejected your fly. It had a good look at your fly and decided against eating it. It may have seen you standing there and changed its mind about feeding. When a trout rejects a fly pattern, then no matter how you present it again, this fish is not going to take that fly. You have to change the pattern. Or, rest the fish and come back later (by later, I mean about 15 minutes. Don't wait too long. Sometimes when you show a fly to a trout and take it away, it will think about that fly it saw. Then, you show it again and take it away, it really thinks about the fly it saw. This is like playing the string game with a cat. Eventually, you will entice the trout enough that it can't resist pouncing on that fly.)

SETTING THE HOOK AND LANDING A BIG FISH

THE SET

Lift the rod. There. That's it. That is the set. Trout are not bass. They are not Walleye or halibut or catfish. Those other species are tough fish with huge strong jaws and fat lips. Trout are delicate. If you see any kind of disturbance on the surface of the water where you think your fly might be, then swiftly lift your rod to shoulder height. Look for your fly. Ideally, you need to have the line under constant light tension with your free hand, like this:

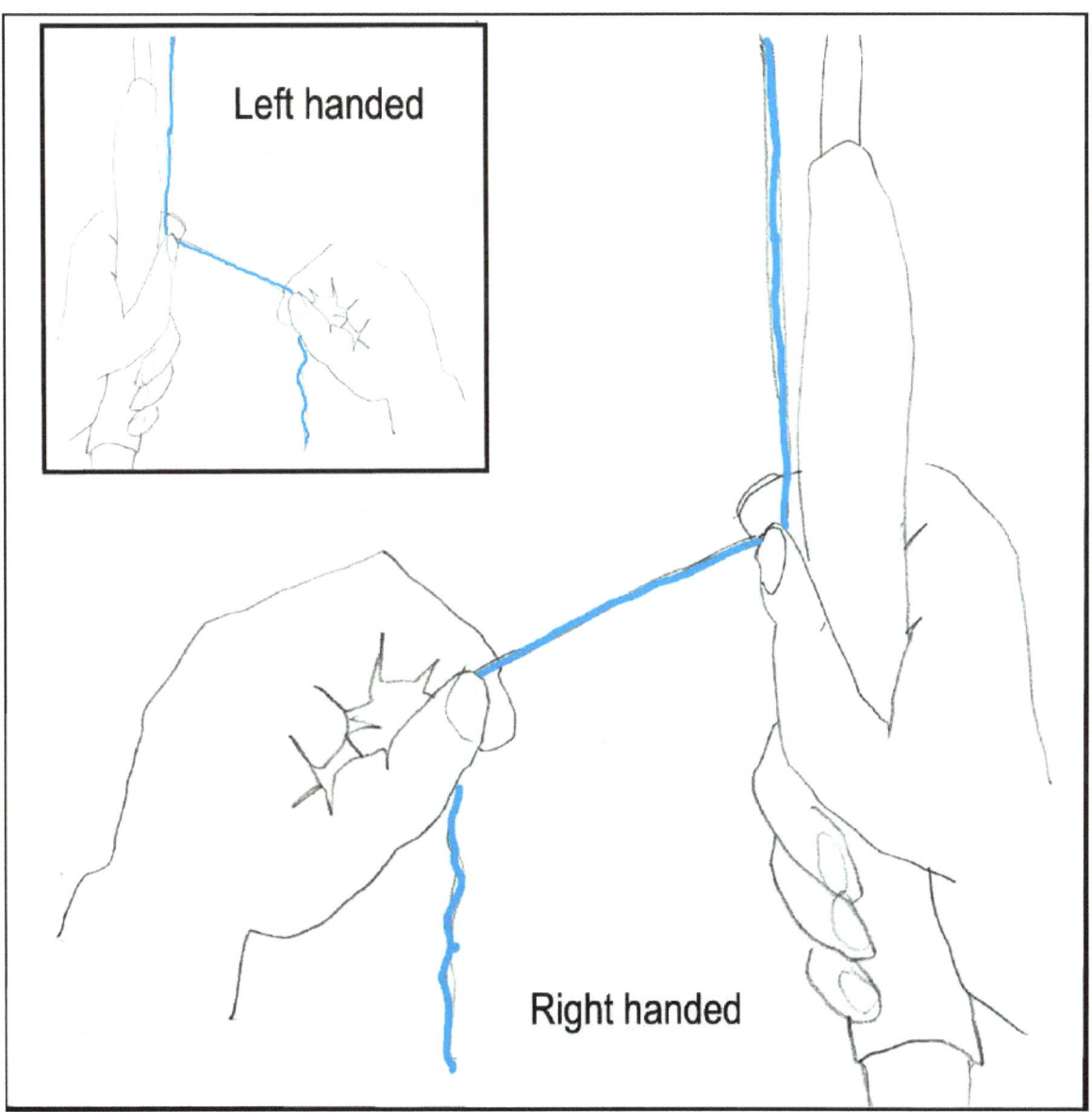

Figure 25 Line control: trap the line with the trigger finger on your rod-holding hand and hold the excess line in your free hand. Keep slight tension on the line.

SETTING THE HOOK AND LANDING A BIG FISH

This way, with constant slight tension, the line and hook move when you lift the rod. There shouldn't be so much slack in the line on the water that you have to strip strip strip[18] just to get the extra line in before the hook will turn. When you lift the rod with the line trapped by your finger(s), either the pattern comes skating toward you empty, or there is a BANG BANG BANG on the end of your line because a trout is shaking its head underwater trying to free itself. (Or, one bounce and the trout is off… Or, a stiff sudden stop because you are snagged…)

Your second move (first is LIFT) is to shoulder the rod with the tip pointing straight up in the air. By this, I mean pull your fist that is holding the rod into your chest up by your shoulder. Keep the rod pointing straight up in the air. You need to point straight up in the air to allow the rod tip to flex and follow the movements of the fish faster than you can react. Let go of the trapped line you're holding in your trigger finger and keep control of the excess line with your free hand ALLOWING THE EXCESS LINE TO FEED OUT TO THE FISH BUT WITH CONTROL.

---

[18] "Strip" or "stripping" means to pull the line through your clamped trigger finger with your free hand. This shortens the amount of line that is out on the water. Let the loose, excess line fall at your feet on the ground or water. That pile of line at your feet is your reserve in case you either have a miraculous cast and the line shoots across the water, or it gets used up in a fleeing trout's run.

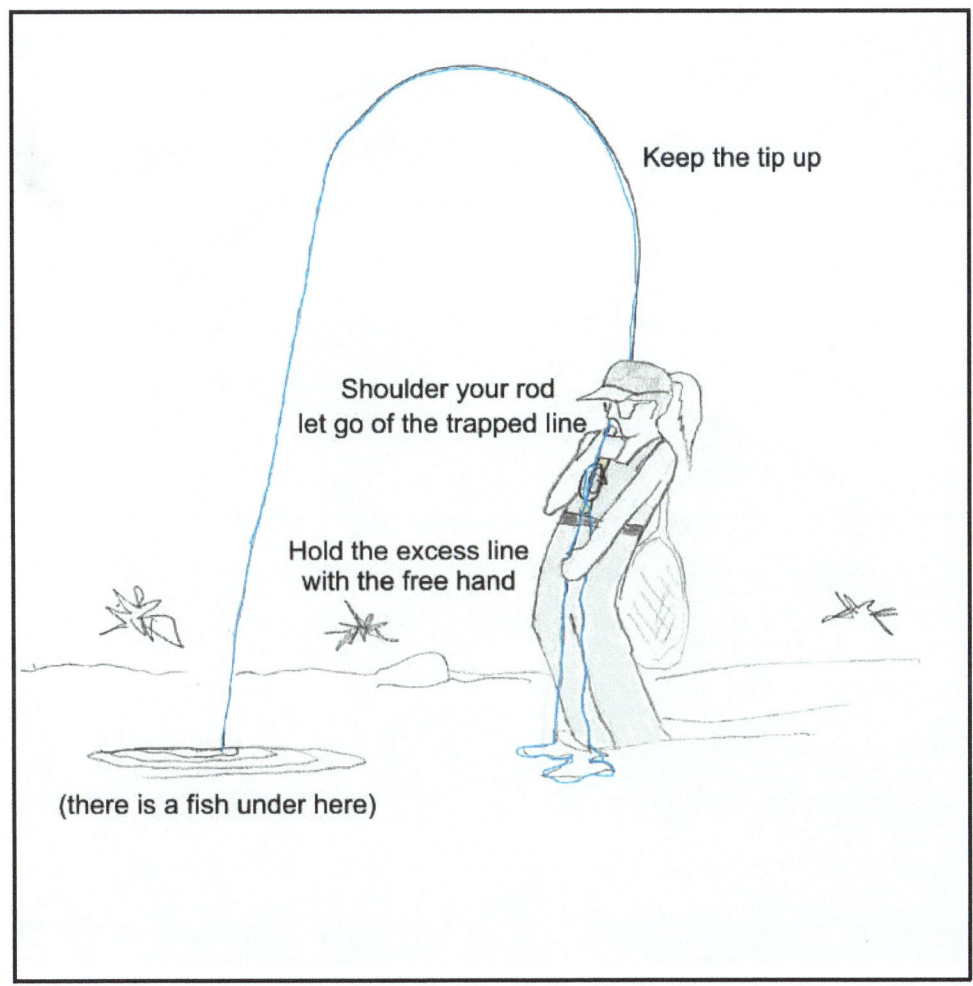

Figure 26 "Playing" a trout with the rod tip up.

You should have your drag on the reel already set in advance so that the trout can pull line off and run with ease but not so loose that loops come flying back around onto the reel backwards. You can cup the reel with your free hand so as to slow the unspooling down but still allow the line to come off evenly. Keep the tip up in the air. Keep the rod clutched to your chest. Line with tension, maybe unspooling if the trout is fleeing. That's the game.

Ideally, you will want to reel in the slack and "get the fish on the reel". You have to do this a little at a time, both letting the fish flee (unspool) and alternatively cranking away at the reel when the trout allows you to nurse it closer (or if you are walking into the trout following it downstream). Back and forth. Run a little, reel a little. Get the fish on the reel.

SETTING THE HOOK AND LANDING A BIG FISH

LET THE FISH BE A FISH

There are different behaviors for trout when they get hooked. Oddly, some species have characteristic responses. Big Brown trout tend to dive. Their goal is to wipe their face on the bottom of the stream or against submerged debris, just like birds do to clean their beaks by wiping their beaks on branches. (Did you know birds clean their beaks on branches? Well, they do…) Rainbow trout often leap clear of the water and make a run for it. I've seen rainbows tumbling across the surface of the water doing cartwheels like whirling dervishes. (Thus, the name of my fly shop: Tumbling Trout – named after the behavior of rainbows on the Big Horn River in Montana.)

If a trout wants to dive, gently but firmly keep its head up – don't pull it to the surface. Let it be a fish. Just keep its head from going any deeper. Let the rod tip bounce up and down to respond to the trout's attempt to dive. Keep the rod shouldered. If you come to a stalemate, the trout might be in a frustrated state of lock-up, that is, it is holding its nose against the pull of the line with intent to dive but in a static state. It can't go any deeper because you are holding its nose up. Let it sit like this a moment and allow it to gently keep tugging downward. This is a good time to slowly and gently try and lead the trout sideways to shallow water. This is a good time to reel in the excess line, too. Get it on the reel. Don't try to pull the trout up. Nurse it sideways. This action will likely trigger the trout to try and dive again. Just repeat this process with patience. The trout is exhausting itself trying to dive but you won't let it. You will win. Let it run, reel it back. And so on.

This stalemate is a good time to assess your surroundings. Look for a shallow place downstream that you can enter the water safely and/or kneel to net the fish. If you can urge the fish to move downstream, you have an opportunity to shorten the distance between yourself and the trout by pulling it to the nearest bank and reeling the excess line in. If the trout turns downstream to run, keep the rod shouldered and the tip up. Let it run. Sometimes, I extend my arm and hold the rod out in front of me. I keep the tip up and I keep track of the degree to which my rod is bent. I might use two hands to hold the rod out, so the tip stays up because a large trout is heavy. I may have to gently feed line out through my fingers in order to relax the apex of the bend in the rod to prevent the rod from shattering.

GET THE TROUT ON THE REEL

If you have a chance during a stalemate to reel in the extra line, then do so. Getting all the line spooled onto the reel allows the rod and reel to operate with maximum efficiency that they are designed for. (This is where you can really tell the different between a $80 set up and a $600 set up. Rod response and reel drag make a world of difference when you are fighting a big trout.)

THE FINAL BUCK

If a trout wants to run, let it run. Let the line unspool with the drag set to retain minor tension but to unspool with some degree of ease if the trout tugs. (If the reel just unspools freely, the line will come around the arbor too fast and get caught up in a backwards-spooled loop on the reel and you'll have a hairball.) If a large trout has not run yet, I usually move into it and encourage it to run. A big trout should be urged to run at least once. If it is stubbornly holding to its spot and not letting you guide it into the shallow water, or if it is still bucking and trying to flee, then it still has enough energy to give a final buck at the rim of the net and get off the hook. It's better to let the fish be a fish and to trust the rod and reel and play the trout rather than to muscle the fish over to the rim of the net just to have it buck and break off.

There are some physical mechanisms going on with your gear that you need to understand. The rod is designed to respond with flexure at the action of the trout. The line is elastic. The leader and tippet have tensile strength. Your knot is based on proven tests. If you interrupt or impede any of these aspects, you will give the trout an advantage. It will buck off the hook or break the leader / tippet / knot. Here are some to-do's and some do not's:

DO

- Hold the rod tip up up up to allow the rod to move within its maximum range of motion and rebound;
- Reel the spare line in and allow the drag setting to either keep tension or to unspool with control;
- Keep the leader / tippet clear of obstacles – don't touch this;
- Tie a good knot. Check your knots twice.

DON'T

- Point at the fish or lower the rod tip (this limits the ability of the rod to rebound and flex)
- Pinch or hold the line taut (the line will jerk and cause a hiatus in the tension, which the trout can use to throw the hook)
- Touch the leader or tippet (this will give the trout a point of leverage where it can use its weight to snap the line)

Once the trout is moving, you've got to match its pace – go where the trout goes. Let it lead you. Follow the trout, push it onward. Pressure the trout to move but don't get in front of it when it flees. Control its head. Keep your rod tip up and direct the trout's head toward one bank or the other. If you control the head, you control the fish. The trout will eventually become passive. You've got to encourage it to run, maybe twice. If it's a big trout (20 + inches) you might even pressure the animal to run three times depending on its verve. Direct it to the left. Redirect it to the right. Again and again. I may let a big fish rest a little bit between runs and then pressure it again. The urging of the run is to train the trout that you are in control. You let it rest a moment. You pressure it. You let it rest. You pressure it. POOF! It's trained. It will become passive.

THE NET

Get a net to fit the size of fish you're are going for before you go fishing. Get a rubber bag net. The mesh ones remove the trout's protective slime and snag your flies. The nets made out of string will "gill" the trout – that is, the strings sweep inside the gill plate, destroying the gills and the strings rake the trout body. That is a slow and agonizing death for a fish. Invest in a both a big and a little net both with rubber baskets.

LANDING A TROUT

When you have played the trout to the point it allows you to guide it to shallow water, get the net ready for placement while keeping the rod tip up. The trout should be "on the reel" rather than being held on the line with a pinched hand. The line's length has to be shortened enough so that the fish is within netting distance. Unfortunately, this sometimes means that the line and part of the leader are inside the guides, which limits the elasticity of the line and makes a leverage point that the trout might break off. That's why you shouldn't try to net a bucking fish.

When the trout becomes passive, it is ready for the net, which has to be presented from under the water and from downstream – tail going into the net first. Lower a trout tail-first into a net by lowering the rod. Don't ever go for the head of the trout with the net. The net has to come to the fish from downstream with the head of the trout facing upstream. If the trout is facing downstream trying to flee you, then you haven't played it enough. The trout has to be passive and facing upstream before it is ready to be netted. The same goes for trying to net a fish from the side. For every lunge with the net at the side of a trout, you'll be making swipes at an ever escaping trout. The trout will win.

Hold the net under the water downstream of the trout and feed the passive fish tail-first into the net. If the trout is not played out, it will give another buck right before you scoop the net around it. This last buck often results in the trout breaking the tippet because the rod is at maximum apex and the trout can yank against that tension to produce a rupture.

SETTING THE HOOK AND LANDING A BIG FISH

Keep an eye on the apex of your rod tip. If the rod is at its maximum bend, then one more buck from the trout might shatter the rod. If the rod is at maximum bend, let some line out and hold the rod out to your side to provide some relief on the angle of bend. You'll still have to maintain the tip pointing back in order to allow the rod to flex.

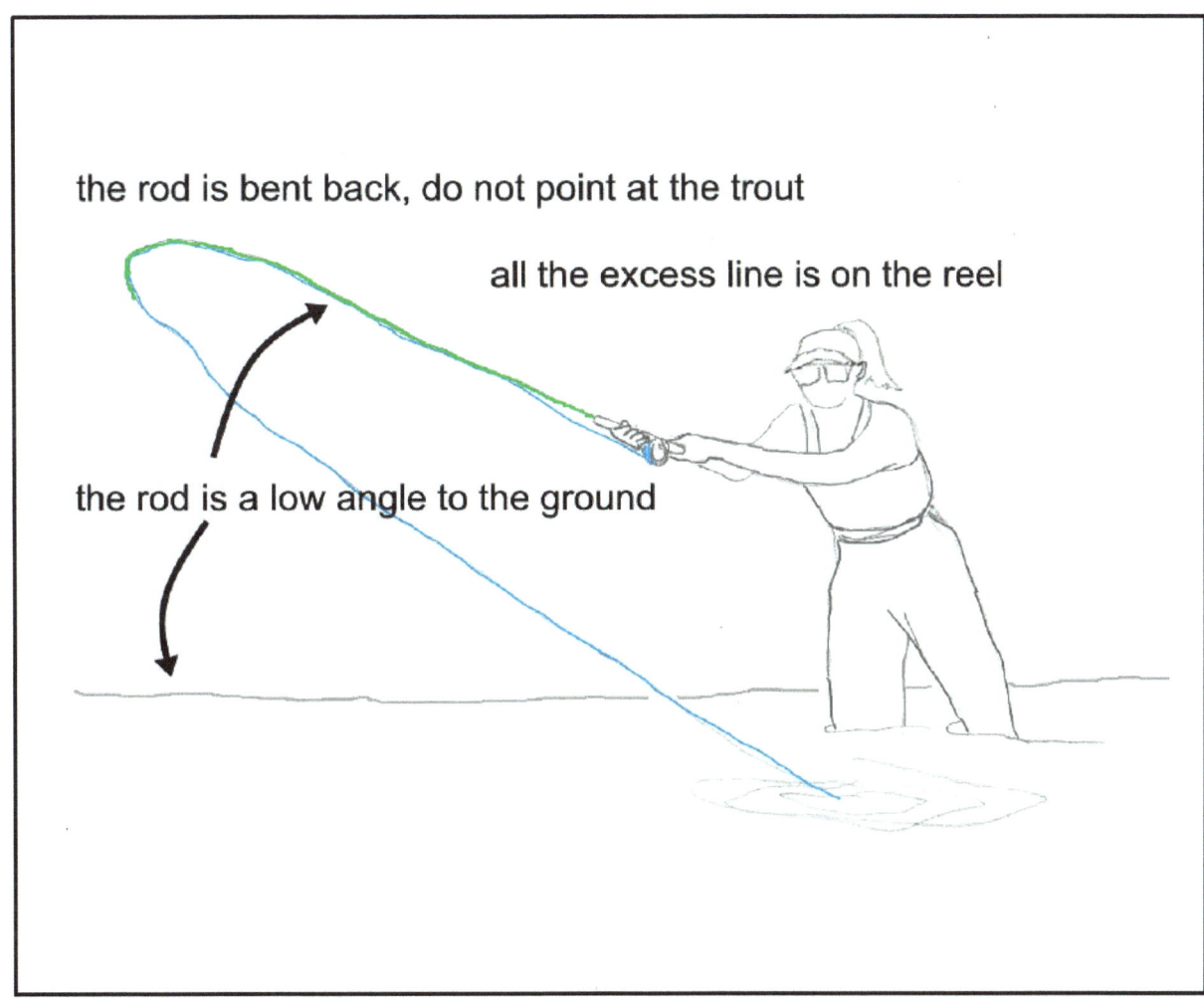

Figure 27 Holding the rod out to your side will relax the bend in the tip.

If the rod has any kind of play left in the bend, the movement of the tip will compensate the thrashing fish and it won't be able to break the tippet. That said, it is important to scoop the fish with one fell swoop completely swinging upstream beyond its snout so as to accommodate any last minute surge in the fish (or wavering of your stance). Scoop forward and up. If you aren't close enough to scoop forward and beyond the trout's snout, then you have to get closer. The trout is going to lurch forward, so you really have to have enough room to over-shoot its head in the scoop. Don't be afraid to re-work a large fish before netting it if it is too energetic to land with care. If you tried to net it and it took off again, re-play it just as before. Utilize your unending patience. You are very patient; didn't I tell you that earlier? You are more patient than a trout.

And this, my friends, is why it is good form to allow someone with a big fish on the line to have the right of way. Helping to net a big fish will drastically improve the trout's survival. Think of the fish: help the other guy.

UNHOOKING THE TROUT

Don't touch their gills. Just don't. Once I've got a big fish in the net, I clasp the top of the net shut over the top of the trout so it can't escape. Tuck yer rod under yer arm to free up both hands. Lower the net into the water, so the entire fish, but most particularly, the fish's head and gills, are completely submerged. Dip your hands in the water to get them wet <u>and cold</u>. I organize my stuff quickly in this situation. I might put my rod down. I might just tuck my rod under my arm pointing backwards. I grab my hemostats and open them, and then prepare to remove the hook. The best way to remove a hook is to crimp the barb BEFORE YOU EVEN START. Clamp the hemostat onto the shank of the hook and let the fish pull itself off the fly. You don't need to grab or squeeze the fish. Just grab the shank of the hook with the hemostat. I've found that if the fish pulls itself off the fly, it has a sense of relief and this kicks in an automated response to thrive. Instead of being dizzy, the fish that frees itself will usually regain its senses and become reoriented to what is up or down. With the fish free of the hook wiggling in the net and partially submerged in the water, I can prepare a camera (or not, I seldom photograph a fish unless something about it is unusual like the coloring or the species I want to document.)

NOTE: A belly-up fish in the net may be more passive and easier to unhook. However, it is dangerously close to slipping into a merciful state of shock, as nature has built into animals, to avoid the stress of pain or terror. Don't keep a trout belly up for long and I'm sure to rest it dorsal up until it recuperates.

THE PHOTO OF GLORY

The best way to capture your animal for posterity sake, is to enhance its color and girth in its natural habitat with as little stress to the trout as possible. There are tricks to this. Foremost, the trout's status is more important than a photo. Is it energetic or stunned? Do you need to let it resuscitate for a minute? Do you need to simply let it go immediately? You need to keep the animal submerged as much as is possible. In most cases, you don't have to lift the fish with your hands at all. Why might you opt for this?

The skeleton of a fish does not support its body mass against gravity like our skeletons do. The water pushes on all sides of the fish when it is underwater, and it has a swim bladder. It is buoyant. A trout's skeleton is fixed in its tissue to provide rigidity to its body for propulsion. If you were to be picked up by your middle without any support to your body frame, your innards would squish and hurt. It is exactly the same for a trout, especially for a fat one. The bones of the fins are not even attached to the skeleton!

To show the beauty of a trout, lift the net. Make yourself visible in the background with the net / fish held out in front of you to maximize its size. If you use your hand under the net to hold the trout up, the hand and net will show off the size and girth of the fish.

Figure 28 Shirley's first trout on a fly evah! See how big??

A great photo option is to perch the trout's chin on the rim of the net with your hand under its chest and keep the rest of the trout submerged in the net underwater. Photograph the trout's head with the net and your hand for scale and use the water as background. If someone is available to help, try to support the entire length of the trout and keep it in the water.

Figure 29 Supporting a trout for photo prior to release.

IF YOU MUST HOLD THE FISH, GET YER HANDS WET AND COLD. Not only dip your hands in the water but let them soak a moment to get cold. Uncomfortable to you, less harmful to a trout. When lifting a fish for a photo, support it under its chest and rear end, avoid the gills.

Figure 30 Support the trout under its chest and rear. Avoid the gills.

SETTING THE HOOK AND LANDING A BIG FISH

RELEASING THE TROUT

A trout should take itself back into the water under its own ability / control / desire. If it lacks the verve to escape, it may not survive. Your job as captor, is to help the trout become reoriented to its surroundings and allow time for it to resuscitate. To do this, try to keep the fish in the net rather than lay your hot hands on it. Hold the trout upright and faced upstream near the fast, clear part of the current. Let clear water flow naturally over the gills. The action of rocking the fish back and forth in the current contributes to its disorientation. Let it slowly regain its senses still within the net. It is literally dizzy and stressed. You can also let the trout lay between your fingers, which should be open and only providing vertical support still within the net. When the fish begins to struggle, aim its face over the rim of the net toward the center of the stream – to the dark water. Let the fish leave on its own volition.

This type of release triggers the trout's instinct to sense it has escaped and initiates survival mode. This fish is going to sink to a hole underneath the turbulence of the main current and think about what has happened. It is going to aspirate softly and still wobble a bit. Eventually, within 10 minutes usually, the trout will be aspirating with more verve and moving with better balance. It will be a while before it starts feeding again. If the trout is damaged, its aspirations will slow down and its balance will decay. It will begin to slip downstream and tumble belly up until it eventually dies. Think about that, Joe, before you cast a fly in the water. Have a plan for landing, handling and releasing the trout with care before you hook into one. Also, if you are teaching someone to fly fish for the first time, instruct them how to handle a fish BEFORE they lay hands on it.

> *NOTE: If you invest in an underwater camera, recording the underwater release of a fish as it reenters the water and swims off is a very dynamic way to document your experience.*

SETTING THE HOOK AND LANDING A BIG FISH

PART C: GEAR AND RIGGING

1. EQUIPMENT

THE ROD

What exactly is it made out of and how? Why is that necessary? Why does a fly rod cost so much? How do I pick one for me?

Graphite rods are made out of rolled sheets of carbon fiber-polymer. A polymer itself is a chain of molecules - linked carbon atoms. These chains of molecules are linked into long carbon fibers. The fibers can be integrated into sheets – literally, spun like yarn and woven into sheets. Graphite is what we call the sheet that is made out of carbon atom chains. Graphite as a sheet is not very strong, but the carbon fibers are nearly unbreakable. The sheets would tear if not treated. To compensate for the lack of strength as a sheet, the carbon-fiber sheets are dipped into resin. The resin provides strength to the sheet, keeps it from shredding. The sheets are pressed super thin and then heated to remove as much resin as the specific manufacturer has designed for different results. Several sheets of this stuff (the resin-impregnated carbon-polymer-woven-sheets) are rolled together into rod blanks, (Secrest, 2017). During the manufacturing of the rod blanks, decisions have to be made as to the resins. It is the decisions in the processing of the sheet with resin that make for the different physical properties of the rod blanks and these decisions have costs.

Any of these stages in rod blank production can be modified or enhanced to produce different characteristics. The fine line depends on how economical the mass production of a blank is in comparison to integrity for the product. In addition, some rod making companies will mass produce rods, taking lots of blanks and chopping them up and packaging pieces that are not from the same original blank. Some blanks are not balanced well. Some blanks have inconsistent quality from the tip to the butt. That is why fly rods vary so much in cost – the quality varies. By the time you are paying over $300 for a rod, you are paying for a particular manufacturer of rods who has a good reputation for producing consistently higher quality rods, calibrated, balanced, and with a specific action designed into the rods' performance. When you are paying $1,000 for a rod, it better be nice.

I advise people who are perusing first-time rod purchase, *"You won't be able to tell the difference between a $40 rod and a $400 rod until you have built some muscle memory by casting for a season. So, go buy any rod you want. Just be sure to get one with a life-time warranty because you will break this rod one day. If, however, you buy a quality rod from a well-known reputable rod maker, then you will have your first fine rod in a stable of other fine rods you own and use down the road."*

EQUIPMENT

After a person has mastered casting with one specific rod, they have created a base of muscle memory. If they pick up another rod, they will immediately notice a difference. It's only after muscle memory has been created that a person can tell if a faster or slower action rod will enhance or detract from the effectiveness of their casting style. After mastering casting with different rods, then a person can really detect the subtle nuances of different lines. And after a person has the line actions down, they will start to notice the differences in leaders, and tippets, and so on. Eventually, you'll be too old to cast anymore, and you'll have to learn Tenkara... (Hahahhahaahaa)

THE LINE

The fly itself doesn't have any weight (unless it is made to be a weighted fly). So, when you cast, the fly will not pull the line off the reel or even through the guides. The line itself has to be weighted. When you cast, you are utilizing the weight of the line and its velocity to get the leader-tippet-fly to advance over the water. There are different weights of line. You match the weight of the line with the designed weight of the rod. Rod and line weights are based on 1) the average size of fish are you going for; 2) what type of fly method are you going to use; and 3) what is the size (depth/velocity) of the water/stream you are fishing?[19] After you decide which weight is suitable for your fishing purpose, then, you have the tricky choice of how the line operates: floating or sinking?

Fly lines have an inner core and an outer sheath. These materials are flexible and can stretch. The properties of these materials enhance the density, durability, and strength of the line.[20] The core is the material that gives the line its tensile strength.[21] The core is made out of some kind of monofilament or braided nylon. Depending on the properties of the core, the line will behave differently according to temperature, i.e., be stiff or limp. This is a consideration when casting in warm climates (like Southern States of the U.S.) or in the high altitude of the Rocky Mountains of Colorado. That behavior (stiff or limp) is the heart of the fly line. The outer sheath (some kind of plastic coating, like polyurethane, PVC, or other plastic polymer) can have a texture. It can be smooth, slick, or textured (microscopically) for specific behaviors when interfacing with the water. The surface texture

---

[19] Example: are you fishing for your average trout on an average Colorado stream? Or, are you fishing for steelhead on a river in Alaska the size of a glacial flood? Those are some fishing circumstances with different "sizes" of target.
[20] Fly lines actually have to comply with weight specifications as defined by American Fly Fishing Trade Association (AFTMA).
[21] Tensile strength – how strong is it under the strain of being pulled?

EQUIPMENT

of the outer plastic sheath makes the line either sink or float. The microscopic texture of the outer sheath also affects how the line casts in the air or behaves once it touches the water.

You probably can't tell by looking but the casting end of the line (as opposed to the end that you attach to the reel) varies in dimension in order to enhance the cast at fullest reach. This feature is called the "profile" of the line. The line is actually thickened and/or thinned near the fly end in order to enhance propagation of the cast. Here is how this design works:

A fly line has a tapered end (as does the leader) in order to propagate the ripple (wave) of a cast forward in an accelerating loop. When the fly line is fully extended the energy of the cast goes into "turning the trailing leader-tippet over". The loop of your cast is extended overhead as one flat line outward and forward. The choice is, what kind of final behavior do you want a line to produce when you cast? New fly lines come in a box that usually has a diagram that shows the design and offers a description of the intended effect of the tapered end. An example would be a fly line with a bulge designed in the end that tapers down to a thinner diameter. The bulge gives weight to the fly line so you can really ZING it, and the taper allows the very end to gently land on the water without a big thunk. Here is a picture of the end of three fly lines with three different taper designs, but enhanced in fatness in order to amplify the design:

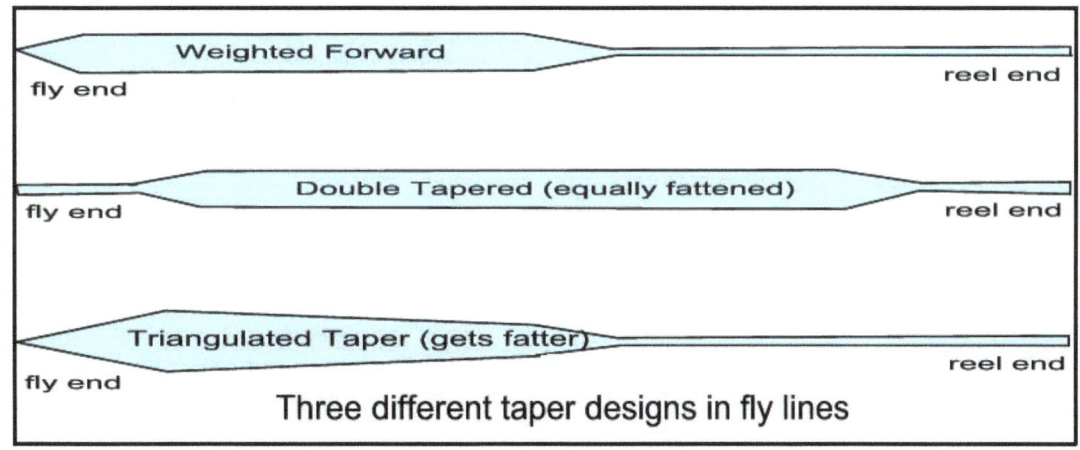

Figure 31 Fly line tapers highly exaggerated in scale.

THE LEADER AND TIPPET

The leader is also elastic like the line. It's basically an extruded plastic thread we call a filament. The material is either going to be "mono" or "fluorocarbon". The mono is a nylon polymer, whereas the fluorocarbon is a polyvinylidene fluoride polymer. The latter – fluoro – is a stronger molecular chain than the nylon polymer.

EQUIPMENT

Mono is more flexible and elastic than fluoro but fluoro has more tensile strength and reflects light the same as water, so a trout does not see fluoro when it is underwater. (Fluoro looks just like water to a trout.) Fluoro costs more $ than mono.

Tippet = same story: mono or fluoro.

The leader provides a less visible part of your rig for getting the fly to the fish. It has a decreasing diameter (gauge) like a bull whip. Did you ever notice that a bull whip has a stout handle and a thinning body? Well, it does, and for a good reason. A bull whip (and leaders) are designed to propagate a ripple from the fatter end (the handle) down to the thinner tip. This thinning in diameter escalates the speed of the wave you created when you whipped it, which increases the velocity, which increases the distance that the end (leader/tippet) will travel forward. Leaders are tapered. They have a certain length and a certain gauge or thinness as is written on the packaging. You might buy a 7.5 foot long, 6x weight leader, for example.

Tippet is not tapered. Tippet is just one diameter its whole length. We use tippet to add to the end of a tapered leader if the leader gets too short.[22] We also use tippet to tie one fly to another fly. (OK, here is some tricky stuff to think about. You can make your own custom leaders by tying tippets together…)

The tippet should be of equal diameter or one step thinner than the gauge of the leader, i.e., gauge-down from 3X leader to 3X or 4X tippet, rather than jumping from 3X leader to 5X tippet. The incremental gauge change affects the cast when the leader and tippet turn over in the air from the fly line during a cast. As you change flies and nip away at tag ends of your knots, the leader will get shorter and fatter. You have to slide your finger down the leader to match the gauge of the leader to the tippet. The length and gauge of the leader should match the –

- Power of the water
- Size of the fish
- Size of the fly

---

[22] Making your own leader means splicing tippet of different gauges in sequence to make a custom leader with the specific length and diminishing diameter you feel you might need to enhance your specific casting action.

EQUIPMENT

VARIATIONS ON A THEME OF LEADER, BY HAYDN (PERSONAL BASSOONIST HUMOR)

- A heavy, fast stream will require heavier shorter leader, like a 6 or 7.5 foot long 4X to 5X leader[23].
- A venue with large trout (over 18 inches) will require a thicker leader (3X-4X)/tippet (4X - 5X).
- If the venue is a tailwater with wily fat trout, then you need a long, thin leader, like a 9 - 10 foot and as fine of tippet as can handle a fatty, like 5X - 6X.
- A really clear, slow part of the stream will require a long but thin leader, like 9 - 12 foot 5 - 6X.
- Venues with really huge trout require 3X leader with 4X-5X tippet. Places where the trout are over 24 inches and the water is deep (like a major river, the Colorado or Big Horn) requires a long (10-14'), fat (4X) leader.
- If the flies are tiny, (many tailwaters fisheries have astoundingly picky trout that only feed on teeny eeny weeny #24 or smaller flies though the trout are GIGANTIC), you have to use a tippet that is thin enough to be obscure to a trout, like 6X, and because the tippet has to fit through the eye of a tiny hook PLUS make a knot that is smaller than the head of the fly.[24]

The tricky part is when there are really large trout (+25 inches) in glassy clear flat water. You have to learn how to control a big strong fish on long thin leader/tippet and how to manage landing it without rupturing your delicate leader/tippet. That is an acquired skill to gain over with time.[25] Fortunately, for Joe, most tailwaters have trout that are used to being caught and released. If you control the fish without bullying it, the fish will probably roll over and ask you to take the hook out of its mouth. True. If you are fishing on wild water and have a huge fish on thin leader/tippet, you are really in for a life-learning circumstance. Be soft. Be patient. Pray.[26]

---

[23] Fast water = short leader – so you can control it as it takes off downstream.
[24] There are varying tensile strengths of tippet. Read the label. It costs more for a tippet that is thin but mighty.
[25] This summary of leader / tippet is generalized. For example, on some incredibly technical waters with huge (35 inch+ trout) you have to use super thin invisible tippet with super long leaders. Those situations require quite accomplished casting technique. Joe Schmo can go for the world's trickiest big fish one day. But today, Joe will use the above reference for beginning his game.
[26] Prayer: the tricky part about praying to win, is that the other contender is also praying. Human: Dear Lord, help me land this divine creature!" Trout: "Dear Lord help me get this hook out of my mouth!"

2. RIGGING FOR STREAMS: THE POINT FLY AND DROPPER

On high pressure waters with picky trout, always use 2 flies one behind the other. One to entice, the other to catch. A trout might actually take the first fly, but more likely, the trout will examine the first fly and decide to pass it up because something about it is suspicious looking. The second fly in close proximity (15-18 inches away) needs to be specifically the right size, shape and color, (in that order), for what the trout are taking. The first fly is for motivating the trout to leave its lair. He'll probably grab the second fly as a consolation prize. Put this in your hat and keep it at hand:

1. SIZE
2. SHAPE
3. COLOR

These are the most significant characteristics of a fly pattern to a trout. (To a fly fisherman, I would say, Catchy Name, Complexity, and Popularity are the most significant characteristics of a fly pattern…)

When you tie a fly onto the end of your leader, that position is called the POINT FLY. Adding a second fly to this rig is called a DROPPER. Most times, we add the dropper directly to the point fly by tying tippet from the point fly (its *barb*) to the eye of the dropper. Sometimes, though, we tie the tippet from the *eye* of the point fly to the eye of the dropper. A less-common variation is to tie a tippet above the point fly, so it sticks out like a "T". We call that a "tag".

NOTE: A "tag" should stick-out, rather than flop if it is tied correctly.

RIGGING FOR STREAMS: THE POINT FLY AND DROPPER

THE THREE PAINFUL KNOTS

POINT FLY / DROPPER (the three most common arrangements)

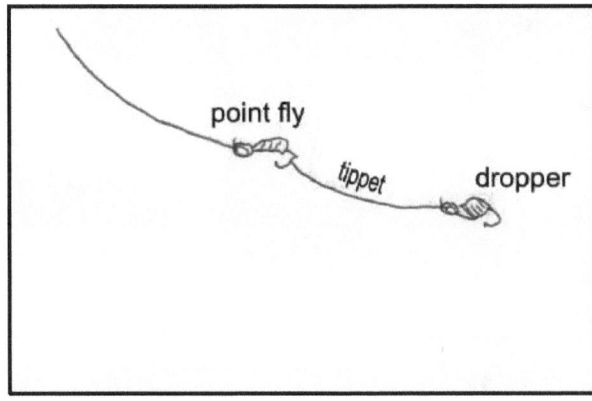

Figure 32 "Barb-to-eye" dropper rig

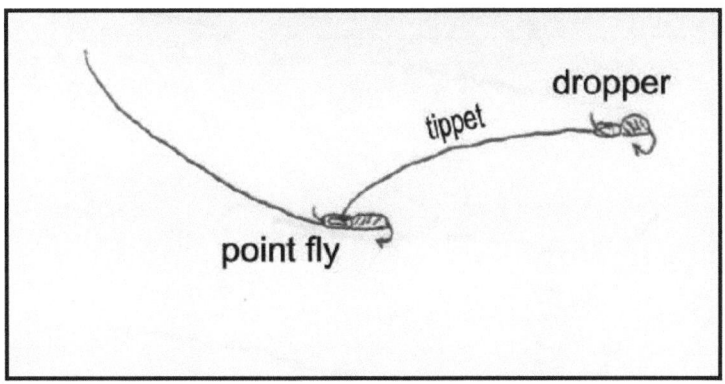

Figure 33 "Eye-to-eye" dropper rig

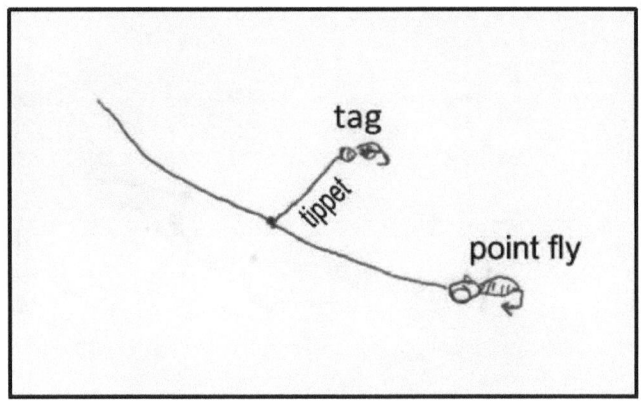

Figure 34 "Tag" dropper rig

RIGGING FOR STREAMS: THE POINT FLY AND DROPPER

Of the three knots you need to tie your flies, the first one is the "Improved Clinch Knot". Some people call this a fisherman's knot. There are A LOT of different knots called fisherman's knot. The one I am talking is this one:

- thread the eye;
- twist the filament back on itself;
- thread the gap next to the eye;
- re-thread the new gap you just created;
- snug it up.

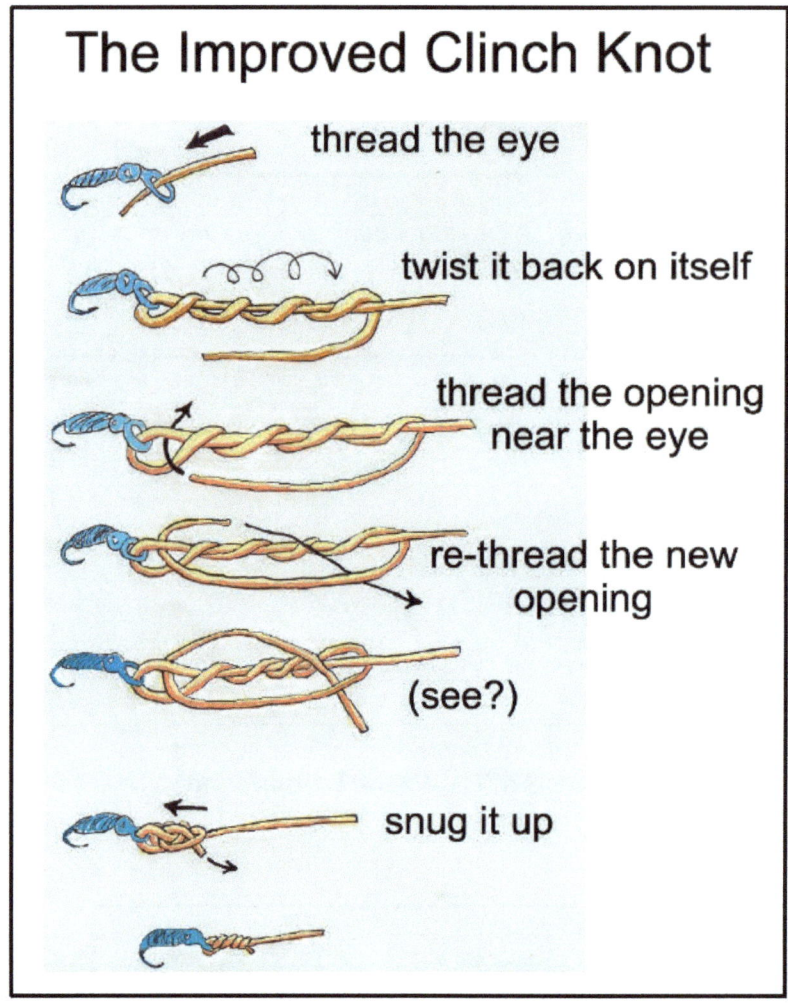

Figure 35 Painful Knot diagram: Improved Clinch Knot

There are many other, useful knots for special effects. Joe Schmo doesn't need to master a lot of knots to catch a big fish. That said, learning and using other knots will enhance HOW MANY big fish can be caught with more reliability[27].

---

[27] You can't buy the knowledge of knots. You have to learn it. Buy a little illustrated book and peruse knots with your friends.

RIGGING FOR STREAMS: THE POINT FLY AND DROPPER

There are 2 more important knots for fly fishing: "The Splice[28]" (for adding tippet to leader) and Phil Iwane's "Knot for the Pathetic Soul"[29] (to make a tag sticking out). Don't worry. I won't make you tie any blood knots. A fly shop should load your new line onto the reel and most fly lines and leaders come with easy-to-use loops for connection.

> NOTE: I have to assume somehow you have gained a leader attached to your line (because I have to assume you have your line attached to some backing attached to your reel…) If not, then please refer to the appendix in this book for those procedures.

Like the clinch knot, the splice knot is a VERY basic knot. You need to learn this knot. It is used to add tippet to your leader[30]. Here is a review of the splice knot:

- cut your desired length of tippet (maybe 20 inches);
- place about 5 inches of tippet to overlap with the leader;
- fold that overlapped portion into a circle;
- pull the free-ends through the circle three times;
- snug it up and snip the tag ends off.

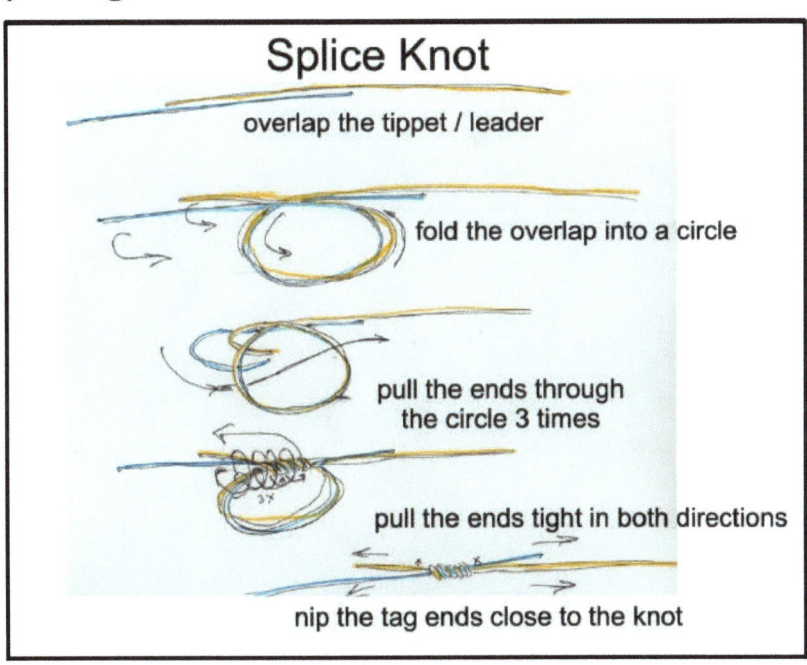

Figure 36 Painful knot diagram: Splice Knot

---

[28] Sometimes called the "Surgeon's Knot"…
[29] Phil Iwane is a Fly Designer for Umpqua Feather Merchants, an Ambassador for Whiting Farms Genetic Fly Tying Feathers, Pro Team Member of the Solarez UV Resins, Pro Staff for the Force Fly Fishing Predator Vises and Dr. Slick. He is known for his extended-body dry flies and most importantly, for his "No Mercy Midge". Plus, he is a good person. People like Phil are why I have faith in humans.
[30] Every time you change flies, you are cutting into the leader and it is getting shorter and thus, fatter. Eventually, you add tippet.

RIGGING FOR STREAMS: THE POINT FLY AND DROPPER

Now, the special AND NEW-TO-YOU knot is Phil Iwane's "Knot-for-the-Pathetic-Soul", which is a variation on the "Dropper Knot". The Knot-for-the-Pathetic-Soul makes a short "tag" of the tippet that sticks out fairly well. We want to use a tag in order to specifically address the way wily trout sometimes bump or detect the leader by nosing at the fly. Here is a diagram of a trout nosing the leader when it goes to take a fly:

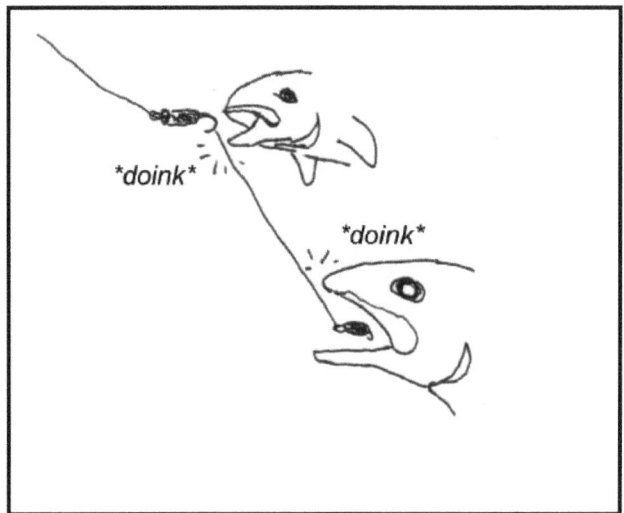

Figure 37 Traditional rig: trout mouth bumps the leader/tippet.

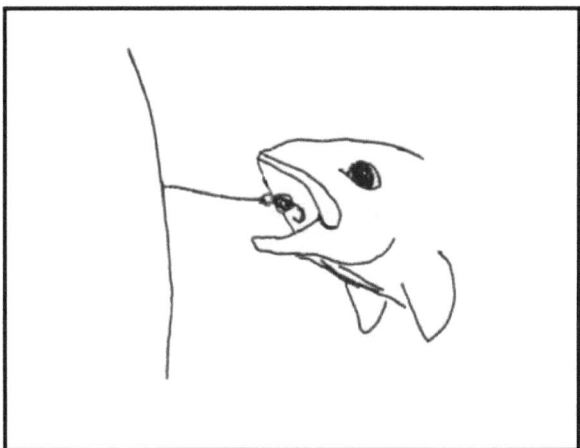

Figure 38 "Tag" - trout mouth encapsulates fly, doesn't touch the line.

RIGGING FOR STREAMS: THE POINT FLY AND DROPPER

OK, here is the painful part – how to tie Phil Iwane's "Knot-for-the-Pathetic-Soul" so you can make a tag:

- Cut about 15 inches of tippet
- Fold the tippet into a circle with tag ends sticking out to the sides
- Hold the top of the tippet circle against the leader

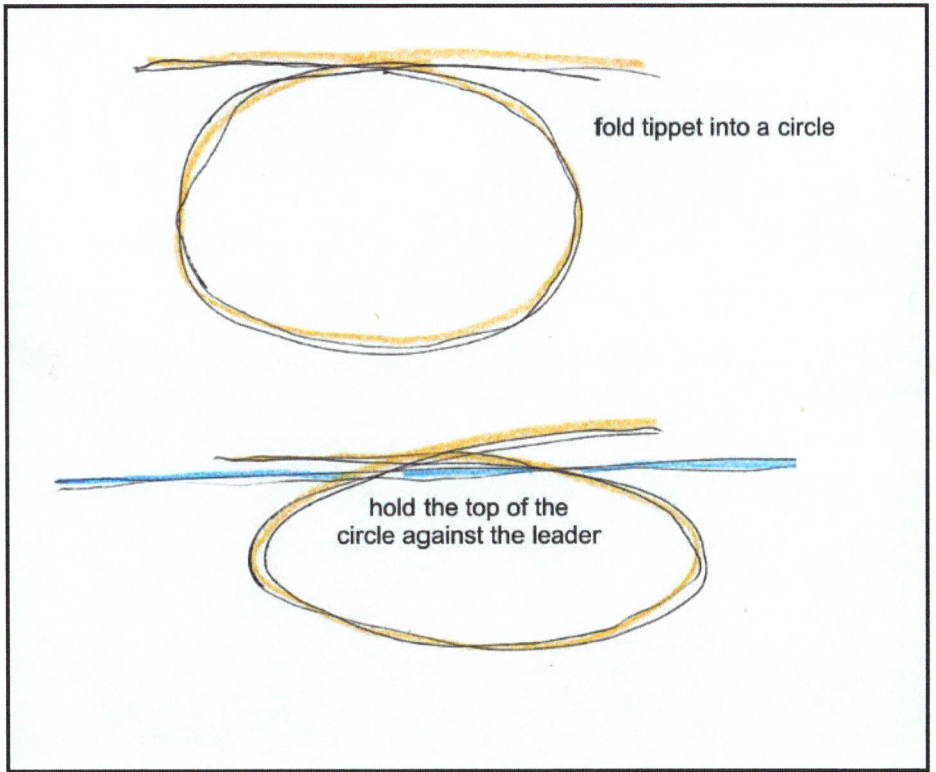

- Wrap the leader around the top of the tippet circle about 5 times.

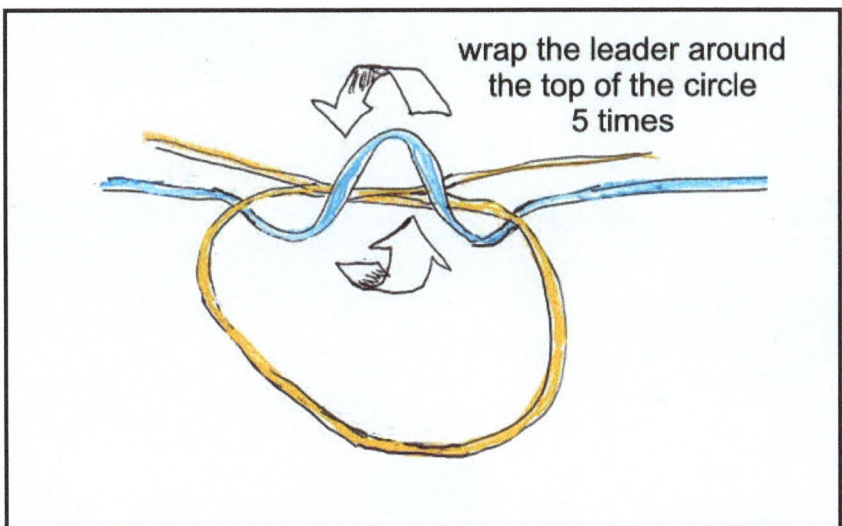

RIGGING FOR STREAMS: THE POINT FLY AND DROPPER

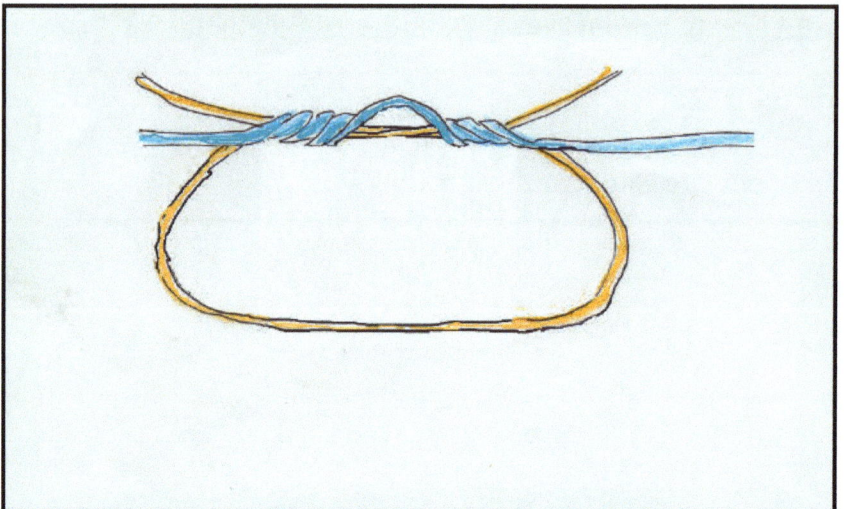

- Reach through the twisted part between the leader and the tippet with your thumb and forefinger
- Grab the bottom of the tippet circle

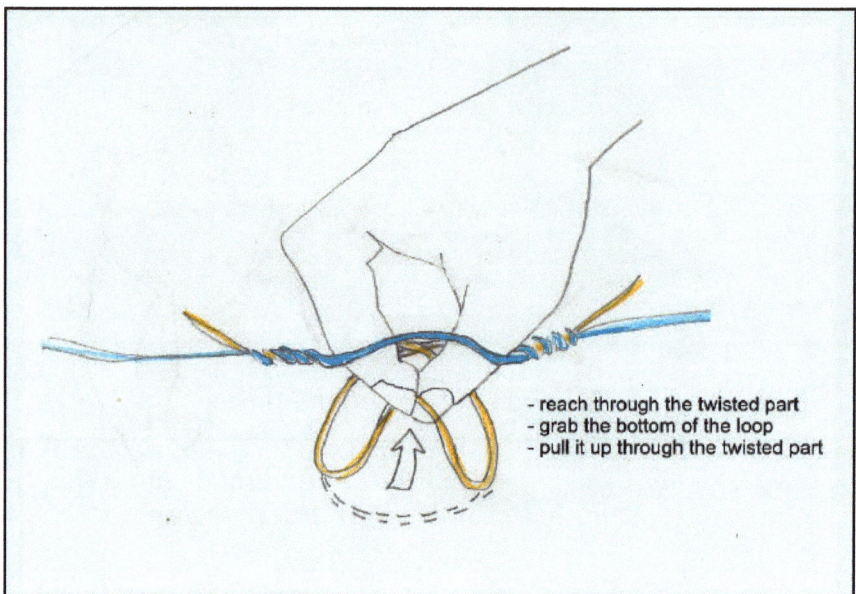

- reach through the twisted part
- grab the bottom of the loop
- pull it up through the twisted part

- Pull the bottom of the tippet up through the opening and transfer this loop to your mouth

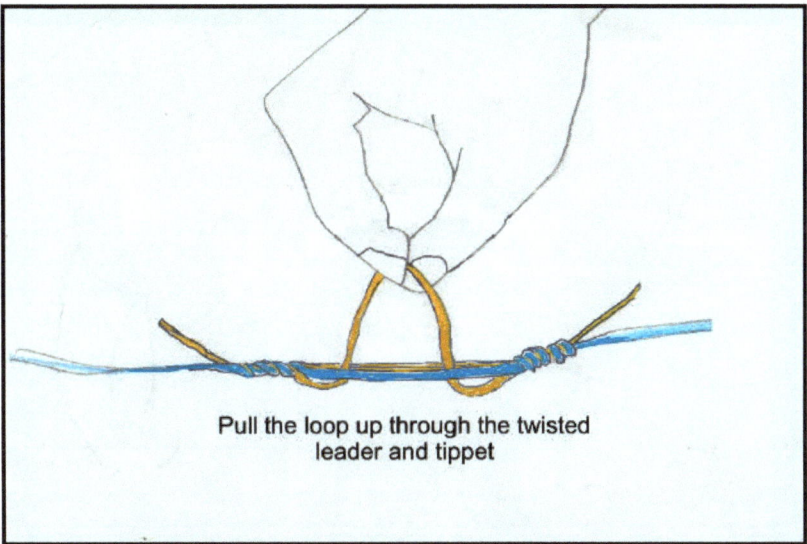

Pull the loop up through the twisted leader and tippet

- Use your mouth to pull on the loop
- Pull both tag ends of the tippet with your fingers to snug up the knot

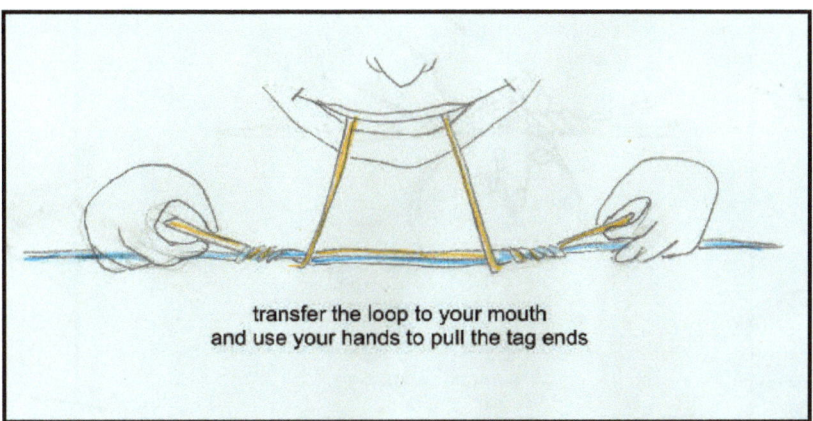

transfer the loop to your mouth and use your hands to pull the tag ends

RIGGING FOR STREAMS: THE POINT FLY AND DROPPER

- Nip the tag ends

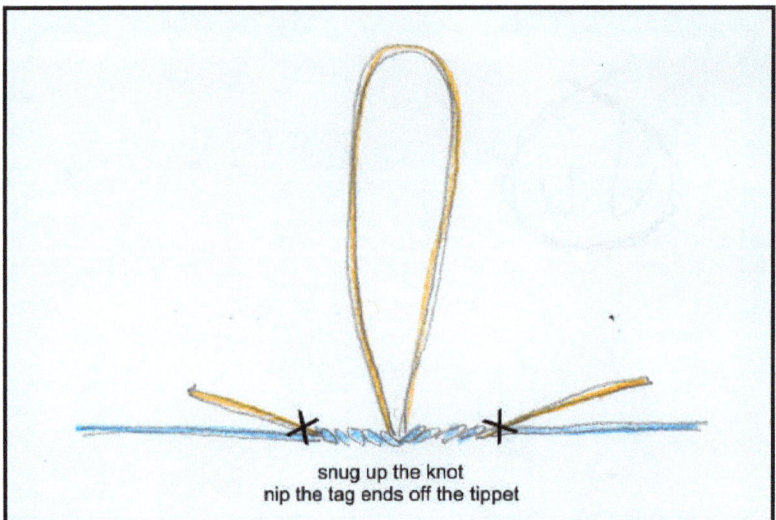

- Cut the resultant loop on the side – not at the top – a little more than halfway up

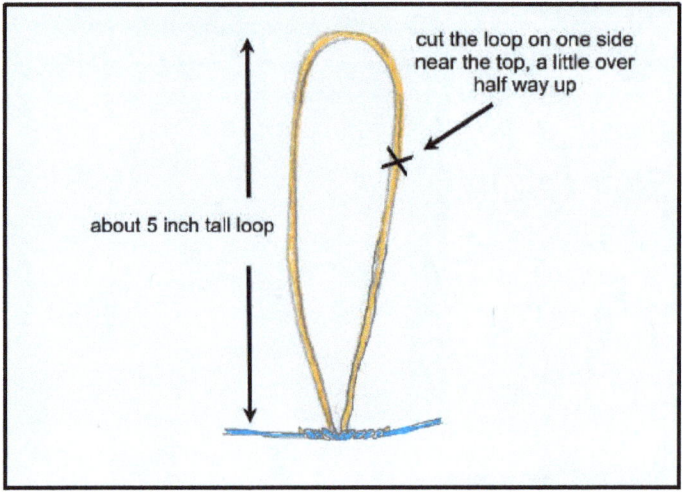

- Use the shorter side of the nipped loop to tie a granny's knot around the base of the longer side of the loop.
- Nip that granny knot's tag end.

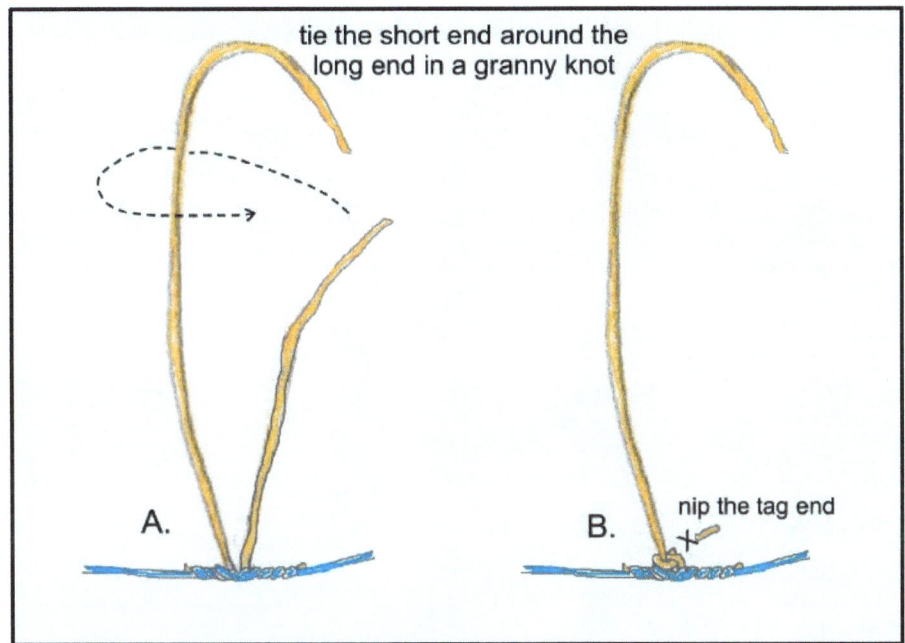

The result is a tippet sticking out perpendicular to the leader with a really good blood-knot-style attachment to the leader[31]. If you really want to ensure that the tag does not fail – apply epoxy to the granny knot (that's what Phil does – he actually keeps a little bottle of Zap-a-Gap in his pocket!). You can make tags on a piece of long

---

[31] This is not a Prusik knot. The Prusik knot would wrap the tippet around the leader. That is, wrap the daughter around the parent. The Prusik knot allows for slip along the parent line. In Phil's knot design, the leader is the parent and the leader wraps around the tippet - the daughter. The leader is incorporated into the knot and therefore, does snot slip.

tippet in advance in the comfort of your home. Spool the strand on a foam reel or put it in a baggie. Later, at the stream, pull the piece with the tags out and splice it to your leader, (or use a tippet ring on the end of your leader!).

If you cannot grasp Phil Iwane's, "Knot for the Pathetic Soul", then relax. Here is a simpler version for making a tag. I call this, "Lazy Man's Knot". It came to me via a Tenkara friend who got it from a man in England who got it from…? I don't know.

RIGGING FOR STREAMS: THE POINT FLY AND DROPPER

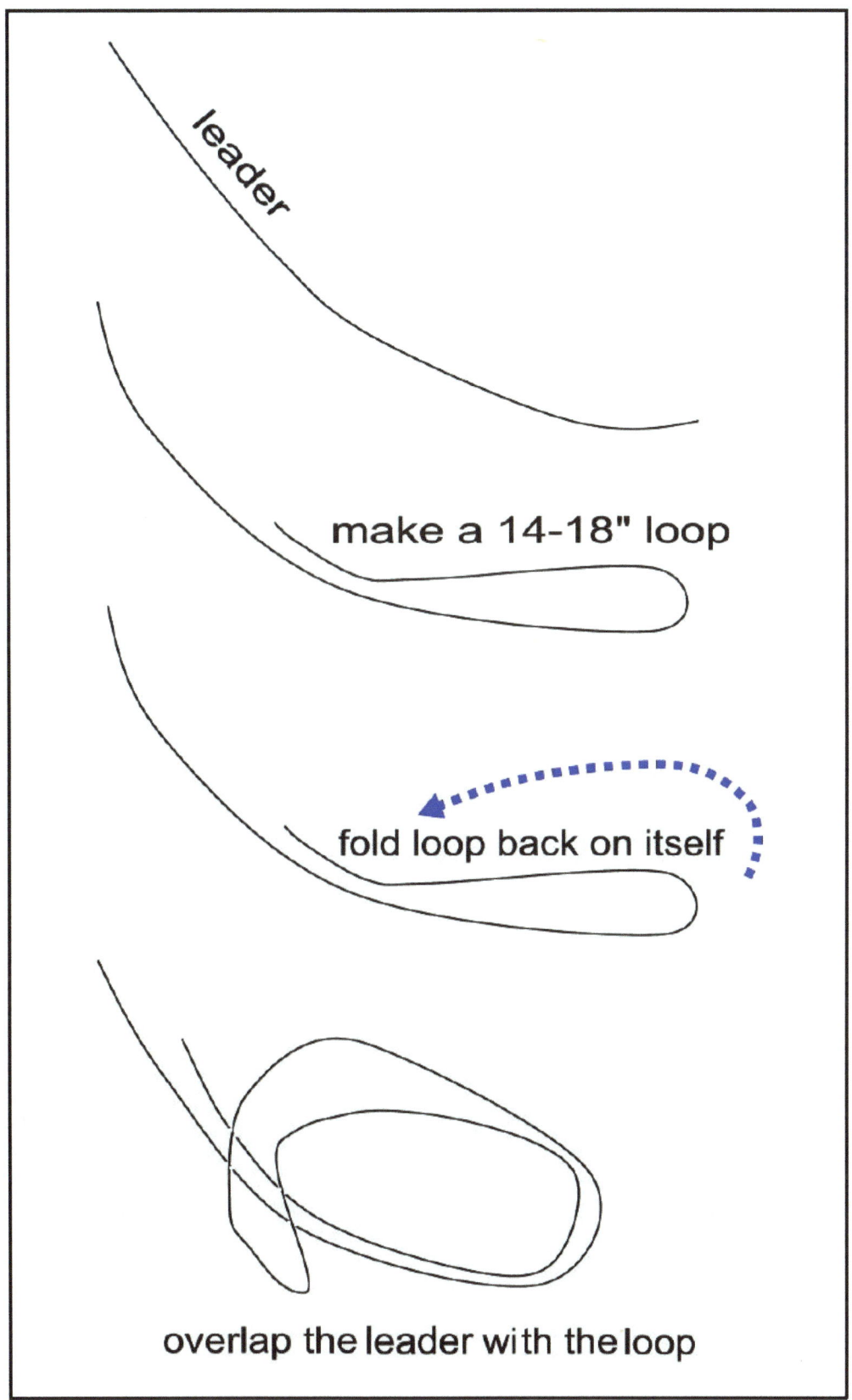

Figure 39 Lazy Man's Knot (Part 1).

RIGGING FOR STREAMS: THE POINT FLY AND DROPPER

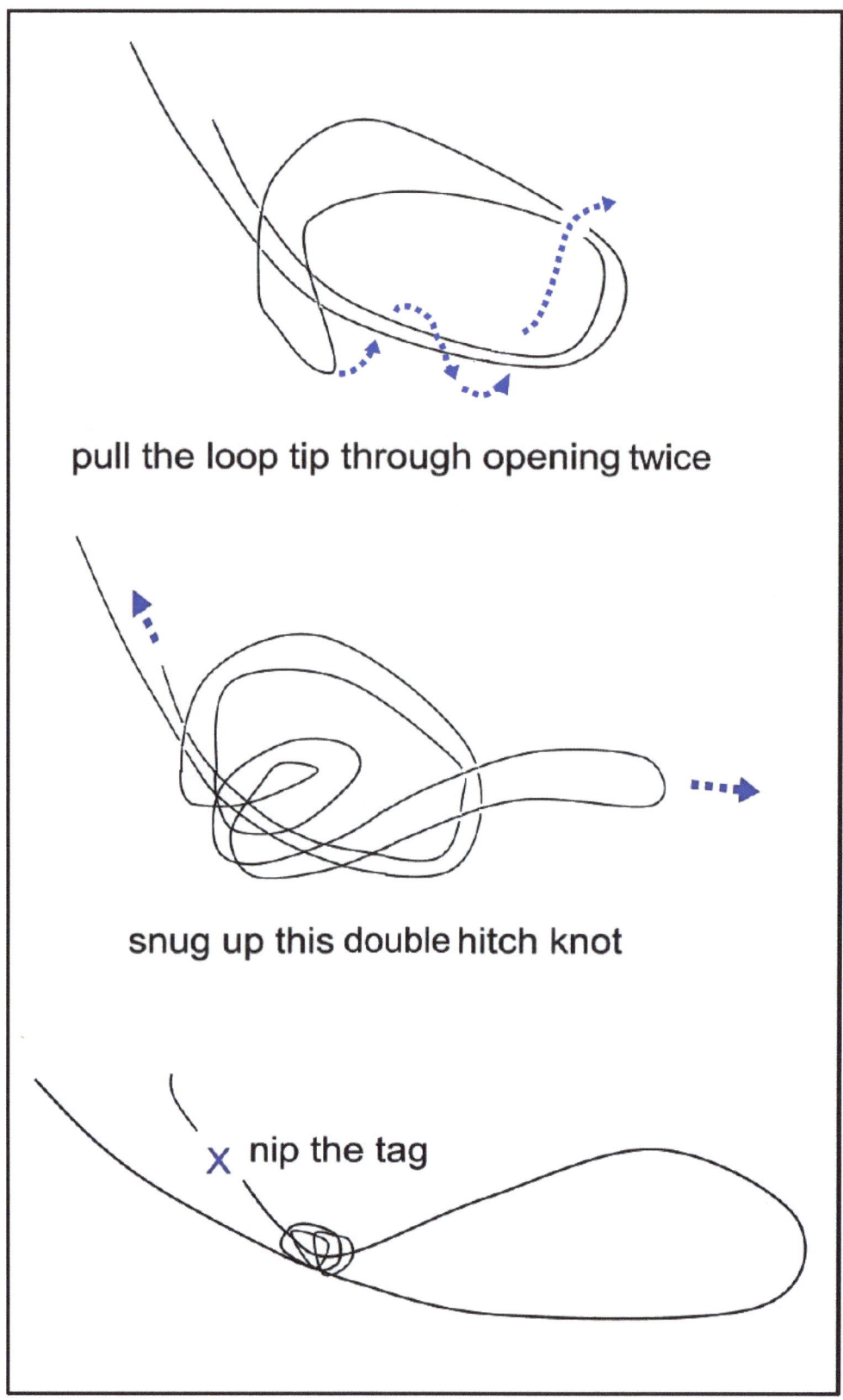

Figure 40 Lazy Man's Knot (Part 2).

RIGGING FOR STREAMS: THE POINT FLY AND DROPPER

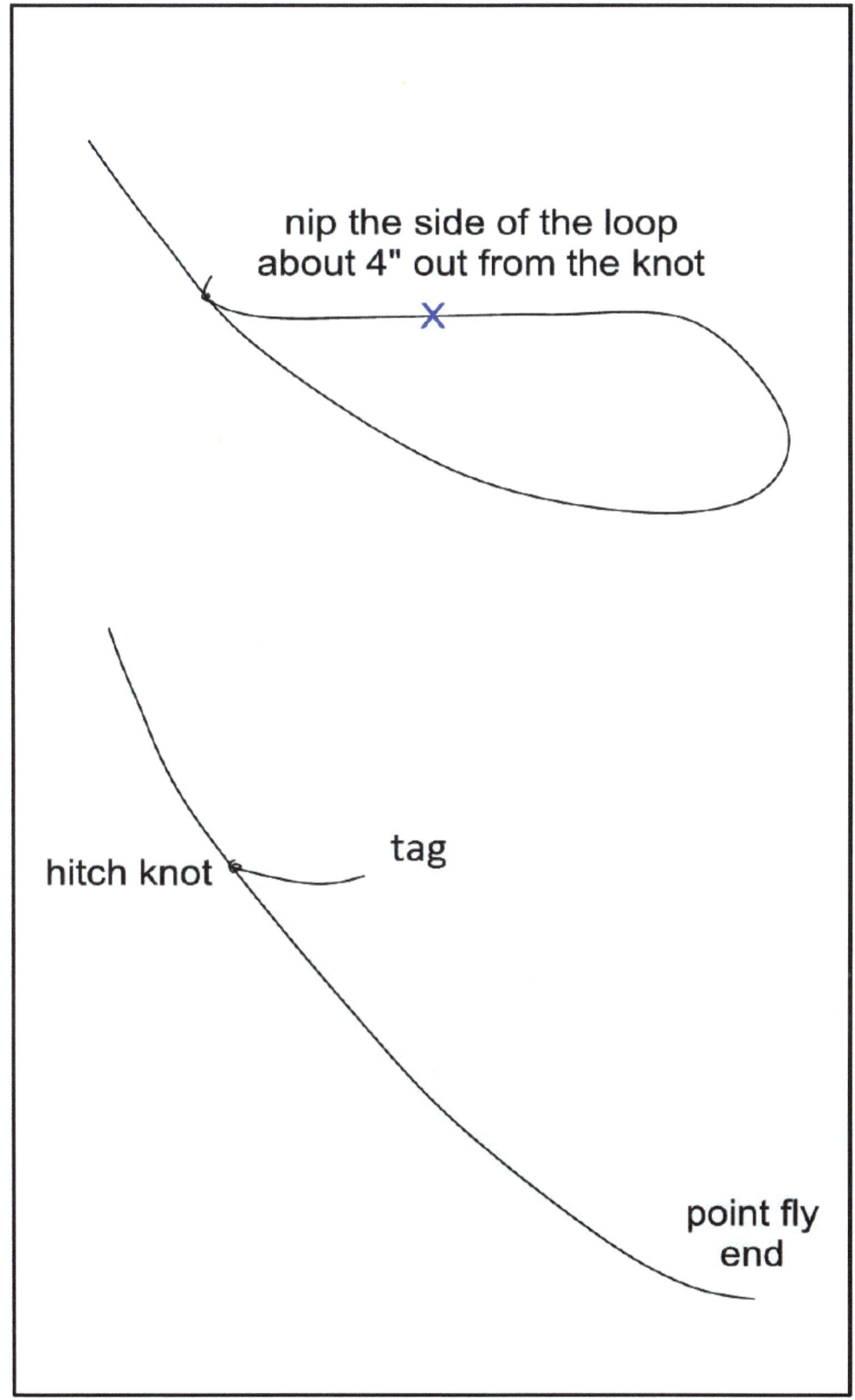

Figure 41 Lazy Man's Knot (Part 3). You better glue this knot.

Figure 42 Remember: No Food for Lazy Man...

RIGGING FOR STREAMS: THE POINT FLY AND DROPPER

THE DRY FLY SETUP

Pretty simple: use 2 flies. Tie the larger of the 2 flies directly to the leader. Thread the second, smaller fly with tippet to the first fly's bend with crimped-barb. (Or use "Lazy Man's Knot" to make a dropper / point fly.)

If the second fly is really small (like a #20 or #22) use a thin tippet, like 5X or 6X, and tie the improved clinch knot with fewer wraps so as to avoid having a knot bigger than the head of the fly. (If you are going to use a super tiny fly, like a #24 or #26 or smaller, you need to use a really small knot, like a Davy Wotton Knot[32]. Joe Schmo doesn't need to go there today, though. Today, Joe can use an improved clinch knot with fewer wraps.

Put floatant on the point fly and slide the floatant up the leader with your fingers. Don't put floatant on the second fly or the tippet. In this way, the second fly might float due to surface tension, but it will eventually sink. That sinking motion often triggers a trout - I don't know why. The sinking effect may emulate a drowned adult or failed emerging adult and maybe that character is appealing to a trout. We can only speculate. As a result, if you time the sinking of the second fly (by trial and error) to occur at the head of a pod of feeding trout, i.e. cast about 8 feet in front of the pod and allow the dropper to start sinking as it enters the territory of the pod. That action has increased the likelihood of getting a trout to select your fly over all the available naturals.

The shorter the tippet between the point fly and dropper (dry flies), the closer the dropper drifts to the surface. The longer the tippet between the point fly and the dropper (dry flies) – the deeper the dropper will drift.

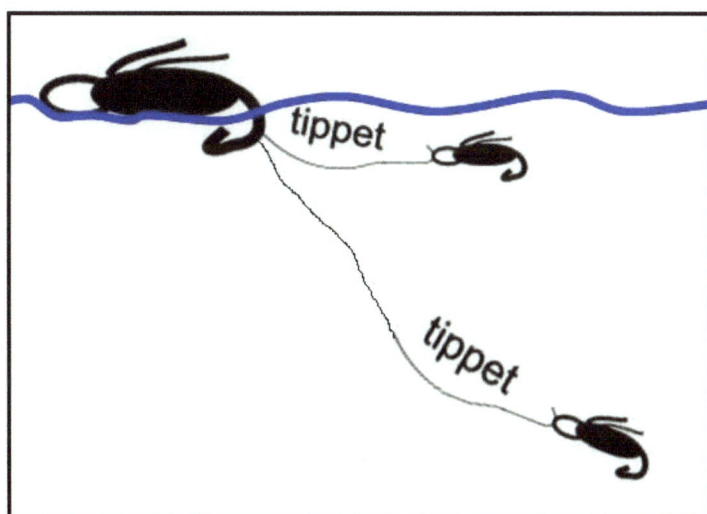

Figure 43 Shorter tippet = dropper rides high; longer tippet = dropper rides lower

---

[32] Davy Wotton is a British fly fishing fly tying guru, a guide, a conservationist, and banjo player. (Wotton, 1995-2013)

RIGGING FOR STREAMS: THE POINT FLY AND DROPPER

THE NYMPHING SETUP

The nymphing rig is a bit more complex than rigging for a dry fly. Still use 2 flies. Still tie the larger of the 2 flies directly to the end of the leader. Still thread the second, smaller fly with tippet. Attach the second fly to the larger fly by one of these three methods: 1) barb-to-eye; 2) eye-to-eye; or 3) attach the second fly to a tag on the leader. (See previous discussion on Painful Knots, above.)

The nymphing rig also utilizes weight to get the flies down to big fish. Either use a heavy bead-head fly as the weight, or add split shot, or both. Put the split shot about 12 inches above the first fly to make the most common nymphing rig. The size of your split shot has to get the rig down but if it is a fat split shot, then it might make the trout suspicious. Start with one little split shot (like "BB" gauge[33]), and maybe add another split shot if that is not enough to get the rig down. *sigh* I wanted to avoid having to post split shot sizes. Here goes:

SIZE	CODE	WEIGHT
TOO BIG	SS	1.6 gm
TOO BIG	AA	0.8 gm
TOO BIG	AB	0.6 gm
USE THIS	BB	0.4 gm
or this	1	0.3 gm
maybe this	4	0.2 gm
too small	6	0.1 gm
too small	8	0.08 gm
too small	10	0.06 gm

Add a strike indicator to the leader below where the line is attached to the leader. The exact depth of the subsurface flies is controlled by where you put the indicator. You can slide the indicator up or down to adjust depth. Also, the velocity of the water will displace the flies in the water column. So, start with the indicator about 12 inches below where the leader is attached to the line. Then, adjust the depth of the leader as you go along by sliding the strike indicator up or down.

You might need a picture to understand all this. Fortunately, I made my famous diagram. I keep it at my counter in my fly shop. I'll put it in this book for Joe Schmo and call it, "Michele's Famous Diagram."

---

[33] As with the gauge of tippet and leader, there are different gauges corresponding to size for split shot.

RIGGING FOR STREAMS: THE POINT FLY AND DROPPER

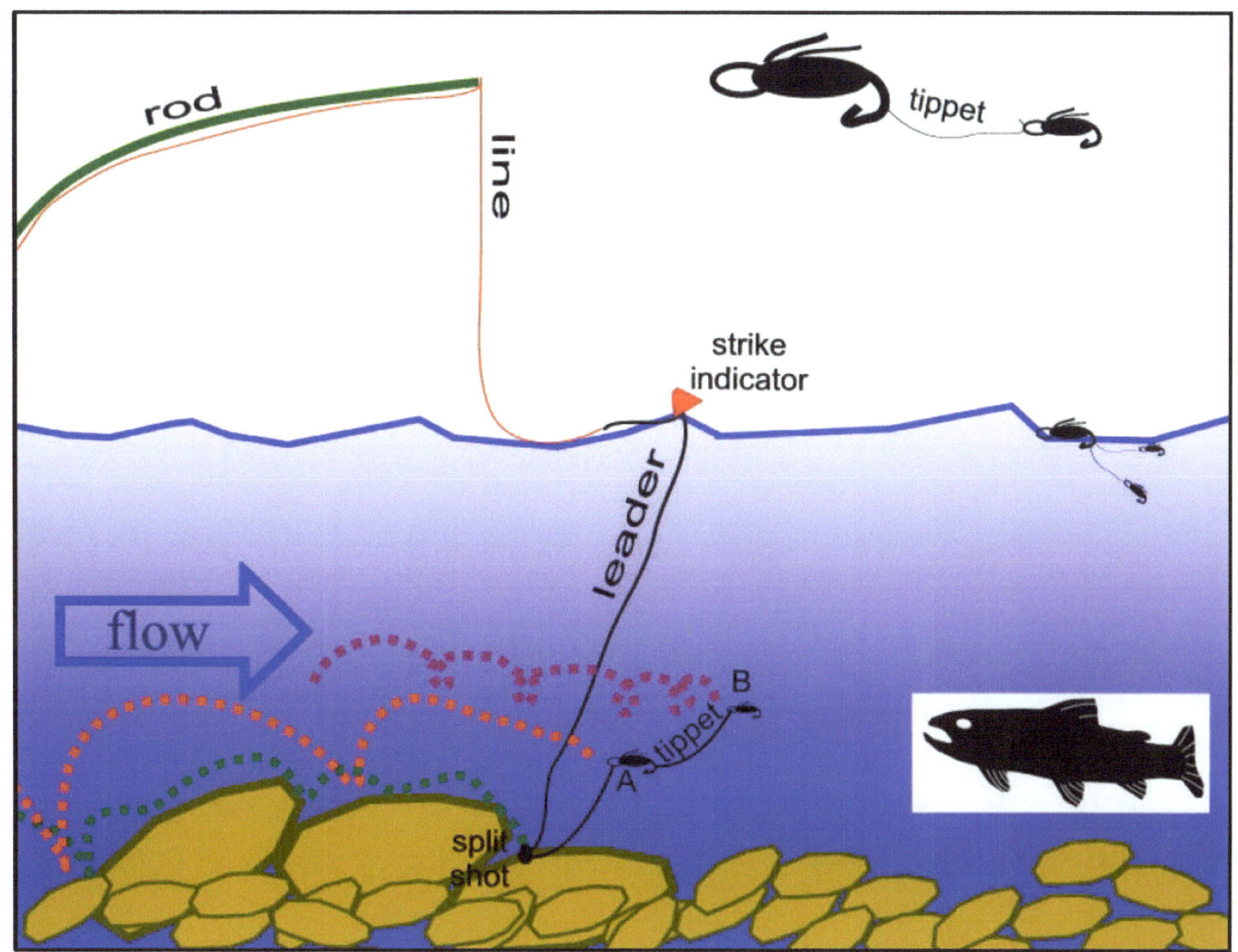

Figure 44 Michele's Famous Diagram

In this underwater diagram, the trout is facing upstream feeding on insects that are drifting down to him. The leader has a big nymph pattern on the end (point fly "A"). Tied to the bigger nymph pattern is a smaller nymph pattern, "B". There is a split shot on the leader above the first, larger nymph fly. Way up at the top is a strike indicator on the leader about a foot below where the colored part of the line is attached to the leader.

The stream's current is pushing all of this rig downstream. The split shot is getting caught on rocks, which makes the strike indicator move. Lift the tip of the rod to lift the split shot off the rocks below. That lift also happens to be "The Set". Lifting the rod gently yet firmly to unsnag it is the correct amount of strength to unsnag a split shot or to set a hook in a delicate trout's mouth.

NOTE: The energy of the set is the same as gently unsnagging a split shot.

Intermittently, the larger nymph pattern will also hit rocks on the bottom of the river. That bouncing also makes the strike indicator move. Keep nursing this bumping rig downstream. That lift of the submerged nymphing rig often triggers a trout to strike. The lift of a nymph off a rock and subsequent free drift is exactly how some pupae move. Sometimes pupae leap in the water column and drift a little way. Trout key in on that movement. When you lift the point fly off the bottom, this motion emulates the natural motion of a pupa with legs, gills, and developed wing sack leaping into the current, as they naturally do to hitch a ride downstream where they can feed on a new area. Trout know what a pupa looks like when it leaps into the current. That is why it is common to get a hit right after you lift the fly. That is also why you keep nymph casting to the same run over and over again – you don't know if you just accidentally lifted a fly right over the head of a trout that was lining up on it.

Meanwhile, the tinier nymph fly (your second fly – the dropper) is tumbling higgledy piggledy in the current. This is emulating a free-drifting pupa caught in the turbulence of the water column, maybe due to some catastrophic event, like a human tromping through the water, or the dam letting water out, or the wind making waves and ripping aquatic weeds loose. Trout are constantly picking the tiny free-drifting pupae out of the water column. The nymph larvae you are emulating with this set up are not very well developed yet. This nymph stage lives between the rocks by scraping algae and plankton off the rock surface for nourishment. Remember: they are not very mobile, cannot propel or swim very well. When they get knocked loose into the current by some force such as your feet shuffling, they tumble helplessly with the current.

When the split shot or heavier fly hits bottom, the strike indicator moves, and you lift the rod. You will either feel a "bang" on the end of the line, because the line has gone taut on a snag. Or, you will feel "bang-bang-bang" because a trout is shaking its head. You've already set the hook when you lifted the rod. Now, you need to begin to play the trout.

What is not shown in the diagram above is the motion of the rig. The water on the top of the stream is flowing faster than the water in the middle, which is flowing faster than the water on the bottom of the stream. This is due to friction. The water on the bottom of the stream is hung up on the floor. The water in the middle is slightly hung up on the slower water at depth. The water on the surface is not hung up on anything. The top of the water is flowing a lot faster than the bottom of the water. As a result, the strike indicator and the colored part of the line are racing downstream faster than the fly patterns.

RIGGING FOR STREAMS: THE POINT FLY AND DROPPER

DON'T LET THE TROUT SEE THE COLORED PART OF THE LINE BEFORE IT SEES THE FLY

To compensate for the faster moving line and strike indicator on the top of the water, either lift the colored part of the line completely off the water and hold it up in the air ("high-stick" it) as it passes by you, and / or mend the line upstream (lift just a portion of the fly line off the water and lay it upstream) – again again again - constantly mending until the flies have moved downstream of where you are standing.

Once the nymphs, leader, strike indicator and colored part of the line have floated downstream of you, turn your toes downstream. Start feeding line out and let the flies tumble downstream. Eventually, trap the unraveling line with your stripping finger to hold it taut. Let the flies swing across the current below you. Wait. Half of your fly fishing real estate is downstream of you. You may get a hit just as you lift to load for the next cast. That's because a rising nymph is stimulating to a trout. This method of swinging a fly downstream is not the same as kicking up silt and drifting a fly to a trout at your feet. Swinging a fly downstream should be way beyond the silt kicked up by your feet. Give the trout some distance downstream. Be a good sportsman.

Summary of Michele's Famous Diagram

- Trout is facing upstream;
- Split shot gets hung up on the bottom, which makes the strike indicator move;
- Lift the line to nurse the split shot off the bottom (This same action is also "The Set" – when a trout takes the fly, you lift the rod, not yank it skyward);
- The larger point fly also hits the bottom, which also makes the strike indicator move;
- Lift the line to nurse the split shot or the point fly along the bottom;
- The tiny dropper fly is rather casually tumbling in the current;
- Mend to keep the strike indicator and colored part of your line upstream of the flies;
- The middle of the stream moves faster than the bottom of the stream, so the line is drifting faster downstream than the flies.

3. TROUBLE-SHOOTING

Things to Test

Sometimes, just changing one element of your method means the whole world to a trout. Some of the elements to change would be in this order:

- Depth (how deep is your fly?)
- Timing (how long is your drift within sight of the trout - 8 seconds or 3 seconds?)
- Action (is the fly at a dead drift or can you give it a twitch? Or, let the fly sink and slowly lift it.)
- Size size size - Leader length and gauge? Tippet length and gauge? Fly size? (Always change down in size to smaller – smaller gauge of tippet, smaller fly, etc.)
- Color (if trout are becoming picky, change to darker rather than lighter.)
- Shape - simply wins. Zebra midge not working? Put something on with a wing bud. When in doubt, emerger patterns are a great go to fly, (except for chubbies - everyone loves a chubby anytime.)

Other variations on your method could mean fishing inside out:

- Cast downstream rather than upstream
- Drift down the center of the stream rather than playing the banks
- Give some action to the fly rather than let it dead drift
- MOVE (go find feeding fish)

Suggestions for Picking Fly Patterns

Ask the local fly shop. They know. That's how they make their living: to know what works. Fly Shops usually post the regional pattern that works best (in their opinion) somewhere on their website. I do so for my region. Here:

www.tumblingtrout.com/fishingstatus

Point Flies

For dry flies, select the larger of the flies the local fly shop recommends like maybe an olive elk hair caddis or blue winged olive (BWO) to be an example of something specific. If you don't have any local advice, then select a general attractor pattern, like a Royal Wulff, or stimulator, or chubby.

For nymphing, select the larger of the flies the local fly shop recommends like maybe a red Copper John or Psycho Prince would be examples. If you don't have any local advice, then select a common all around nymph pattern like a Hare's Ear or a Bead Head Pheasant Tail (BHPT).

By large, I mean a size #14 or #16. Technical water means tiny flies. For nymphing, if you use a large (#14 or #16) tungsten beaded fly for the point fly, then you can probably forgo using split shot because tungsten is so heavy (and also expensive – pay more use less).

These are common point flies you should always have in your arsenal:

- Royal Wulff (dry)
- Stimulator (dry)
- Chubby (dry)
- Hare's Ear (nymphing)
- BHPT (nymphing)
- Prince Nymph (nymphing)

Dropper Flies

For dropper dry flies, try to use the emergence version of the adult fly that the local shop recommends. Examples: an olive RS2 would emulate the emerging adult counterpart of a BWO. A "Chocolate Thunder" or Pat Dorsey's, "Top Secret Midge" will emulate the emergence stage of a variety of mayflies and the incorporation of foam in the pattern also helps keep these dropper flies from pulling the point fly under.

For nymphing, make the dropper fly really tiny, like #20-24, and dark. Zebra midges are classic dropper flies for nymphing. Many midge pupae have a bunch of short tufts sticking out of the head like a crown. Phil Iwane's, "No Mercy Midge" is a great dropper for nymphing because it emulates a midge in the process of expelling itself out of the shuck. Other nymph flies that make great droppers are WD40's for the same reason – the pattern is emulating a developing wing bud. The little dark collars on some midge patterns, (such as using "peacock herl" on "brassies"), are supposed to emulate the gills, or legs of midges. Tiny is the key: these pupae/larvae/nymphs are living in the infant stages of their lives.

Some emergence patterns, like the RS2 or Top Secret Midge, are classic droppers for either dry fly fishing or nymphing as well because so many failed emerging adults become swamped and drown during a hatch event. These patterns of tiny pupa expelling their wings go both ways. They're AC/DC... surface or underwater.

You can also swing wet flies (long, soft hackles on the pattern) or leech patterns (streamers and Wooly Buggers) downstream targeting the base of boulders underwater. You can use these kind of patterns two at a time in tandem (two leeches, or a leech and a soft hackle, for example), as opposed to just one. Add an egg to the streamer and you have created a leech chasing an egg. Put an RS2 behind a wet fly and you have created an interesting (to a trout) snack.

Really old world patterns or patterns from other regions like the east coast or Europe often work really well in a technical water because the resident trout are not familiar with these patterns. Old world patterns include clousers and Mickey Finns... just sayin'.

My personal favorite flies?

GENERAL PATTERNS
Royal Wulff - any size
Parachute Adams (purple) #18
Elk Hair caddis (olive, big and bushy)
Bead Head Pheasant Tail (BHPT)
Parachute BWO
Chernobyl Chubby (purple and HUGE)
RS2 (any kind, I make them out of dryer lint and dog hair)

SPECIFIC PATTERNS
Michele White's "Can-Can Girl"
Phil Iwane's "No Mercy Midge"
Juan Ramirez's "Kryptonite Caddis"
Pat Dorsey's "Top Secret Midge"
Putterbaugh's foam body caddis (black)
Kauffman's Stimulator (orange)
Landon Mayer's "Jiggy Mini-leech" (black or olive)

BIG TROUT OR A SNAG?

Sometimes, a wily trout will investigate a fly and take a pick at it, push it with its snout before taking it. Once the realization kicks in that it is hooked, though, a big brown trout will commonly sink to the bottom of the stream and hold without budging. A big rainbow commonly breaks the surface like a bucking bronco. The situation with a big brown holding on the bottom of the stream is a conundrum. Are you snagged, or have you hooked a big brown? There are some techniques to trying to figure this situation out. First, move into the suspected fish if you can. You want to encourage the trout to flee. If the water is deep, you have to use your body – your feet and shadow -- to intrude the trout's safe space in some way. Splash your feet. Kick water. Get that deep trout to give up its lair.

The difference in nature between your fly intercepting debris in a deep hole or hooking into a big monster trout that you can't see is subtle and can be questionable. Debris will produce one bang and then pull with no dance in the line. A trout will go bang-bang-bang and shakes its head, then rest. A snagged line will catch strands of weed or other debris floating in the water, which produces little bangs, not big bangs. Both sensations feel similar. A snagged line will send a constant vibration up the line, like a radio signal. It's actually producing a

TROUBLE-SHOOTING

harmonic vibration under the water like a violin string. That vibration should be a clue that you are likely snagged deep.

A brown trout might dive or pull across the current. If it moves upstream that is a big clue that you hooked a great grand trout but if you are snagged on a submerged limb, then you might be lifting and dropping the limb rather than playing with a big fish. If you don't know if you have a deep snag or a large trout, play it like it is a large trout. Try to pressure it into fleeing. Keep its head up. Try to feel if there is any indication that the line is moving unnaturally against the current or cross current. Sudden change in direction is a big clue that you might have a gigantic trout on at depth. There is the possibility that the huge fish is tangled in debris, or that you have foul–hooked a fish.[34] If it is *not* foul-hooked, then you should try to work this "fish" until you or someone else can either induce some indicative motion out of the line or make the tough call to cut bait. If the water isn't over your head, then get in the water and kick around the hole. Before you give up, you might throw a large rock in the hole to see if it produces a fleeing trout. Otherwise, pull the line with your hand until it snaps. Don't use your rod to break the line – you will break the rod, either at the ferrule or at the tip. Then, you'll feel stupid.

---

[34] "Foul-hooked" is the unfortunate situation where the trout is hooked on the outside of its body, like a fin or the skin of its side. Your line is dragging the poor animal through the current in the most cumbersome, least stream-lined manner. A foul-hooked fish feels really heavy and its action underwater is hard to read.

4. FINAL NOTES

I am like a trout when it comes to conservation of energy. That said, when I arrive at the river I know I need to invest some time in setting up my rig but I am lazy. So, I usually start with the simplest rig. If that doesn't work, then I get serious about my set up. Here is a common routine for me:

- New leader;
- Start with one dry fly;
- If the one fly doesn't draw some trout action, then add a dropper fly, like an emerger;
- Maybe change my dropper smaller and darker;
- If surface fishing isn't happening, then I change up for nymphing because my extra-long and fine leader has been chopped a bit shorter and thicker as I changed dry flies;
- My initial nymphing set up is "Euro-style" – no strike indicator, no split shot. I rely on sight and feel - using two nymphs, usually in a point fly / tag-dropper array.
- I may change the dropper lots of times.
- If my Euro-method is still not effective, then I will add split shot to fish deeper and a strike indicator.

NOTE: I am a snob. If I am streamer fishing, using a San Juan worm or an egg pattern something has gone wrong. Either the fishing is hard, or I am just too lazy to follow my own doctrine. I don't like catching a trout using these patterns because the trout often engulf – swallow – a worm or egg pattern, which defeats my stalking and hunting a trout.

After I have changed my flies a few times and gone from dry flies to nymphing and then changed those flies as well and added on tippet about three times, I evaluate my kinked lumpy bumpy short leader and if it is under 4 feet long and fat, I change to throwing a chubby. Especially for last cast of the day. When the lighting has deteriorated to the point you can no longer see your fly and your companion is disappearing on the horizon headed back to the car and even the dogs have left, put on a purple chubby and let that go downstream floating higgledy-piggledy where it may, feeding out your line by pumping the end of your lowered rod tip. You will most always catch the last wily trout who has been holding out this whole time waiting for you to go home.

Merrily, merrily, merrily, merrily, Life is but a dream…

The End

FINAL NOTES

ABOUT THE AUTHOR

Michele White lives in the Puma Hills on the east rim of South Park, Colorado. She is a retired international exploration geologist with a master's degree in Geochemistry of Hydrothermal Ore Deposits and a minor in Biology. She worked at the American Museum of Natural History in New York City in the fossil fish department contributing to paleo-fish kill studies. She owns Tumbling Trout fly shop in Lake George, Colorado and is a certified licensed insured and bonded professional fly fishing guide. She has been fly fishing and rowing a dory with her husband, also a geologist, on the Great Rivers of the West for over 20 years. (They are both certified white water boat handlers). She also serves as a Board Member for the Pikes Peak Chapter of Trout Unlimited in Colorado Springs and volunteers on regional conservation projects.

As a writer, Michele White (maiden Murray) is a contributing editor on the masthead for Mountain Gazette, (thanks to John Fayhee). She has been published in Discover the Outdoors, EQUUS, Fly Fishing World, Native People's Magazine, New Tribal Dawn, and The Aquarian.

Her stories (under Michele Murray) are included three anthologies:

- "Colorado Mountain Dogs", published by WestWinds Press, 2014;
- "Comeback Wolves: Western Writers Speak for Wolves in the Southern Rockies", published by Johnson Books, 2005; and
- "Hell's Half Mile: River Runners' Tales of Hilarity and Misadventure", published by Breakaway Books, 2004.

She has three previously published books:

- "Between the Rivers", fly fishing stories with co-authors, Al Marlowe and Karen Christopherson, 2019;
- "Lesser Known Fly Fishing Venues of South Park", a fly fishing atlas for South Park, Colorado, 2017; and
- "Eulogies and Dead Horses", essays about fly fishing and working as a geologist, 2016.

About Michele Colorado Trout Unlimited
- https://www.coloradotu.org/blog/2017/12/behind-the-fin-michelle-white

Michele in PODCAST:
- https://www.askaboutflyfishing.com/speakers/michele-white/

Michele on Tenkara:
- https://www.tenkarausa.com/myportfolio/michele-white-colorado/

Works Cited

Colorado Mountain College - Colorado Mountain College. (n.d.). Retrieved 10 21, 2019, from http://www.coloradomtn.edu

Colorado State Parks & Wildlife Office. (2018). *Colorado Parks & Wildlife 2018 Colorado Fishing Brochure*. Retrieved from CPW Rules and Regulations: https://cpw.state.co.us/Documents/RulesRegs/Brochure/fishing.pdf

Coughlin, D., & Hawryshyn, C. (1994). The contribution of ultraviolet and short-wavelength sensitive cone mechanisms to color vision in rainbow trout. *Brain Behav Evol.* , 43(4-5):219-32. Retrieved from http://archives.evergreen.edu/webpages/curricular/2011-2012/m2o1112/web/fish.html#Notes_and_References

Hamrsky, J. (2018). *Life in Freshwater*. Retrieved from Life in Freshwater: http://lifeinfreshwater.net/scuds-gammaridae/

Heinold, B. (2007). *Mayflies (Ephemeroptera), stoneflies (Plecoptera), and caddisflies (Trichoptera) of the South Platte River Basin of Colorado, Nebraska, and Wyoming, The*. Retrieved 10 21, 2019, from https://mountainscholar.org/handle/10217/38377

Mayer, L. (2019). *Sight Fishing for Trout*. Stackpole Books.

Raupp, D. M. (2019, May). The Bug Guy. (Author, Interviewer)

Secrest, R. (2017). *How Products are Made*. Retrieved from http://www.madehow.com/Volume-5/Fishing-Rod.html

Ulrich, III, A. B. (2018). *A Favorite Fish Food Mysis Shrimp*. Retrieved from Saltwater Aquarium Blog: http://www.saltwateraquariumblog.com/mysis-shrimp-favorite-fish-coral-food/

Wotton, D. (1995-2013). *Fly & Field*. Retrieved from http://www.flyfield.com/davybio.htm

FINAL NOTES

APPENDIX I

HOW TO GET YOUR LINE ONTO YOUR REEL: THE BACKING

The line is expensive. So, "they" manufacture the colored, elastic line to be only as long as is necessary for the maximum cast. A trout may run far down stream, though – further than the length of the expensive line. So, we spool lots and lots of cheaper "backing" onto the reel – hundreds of feet - in case we hook up with a mighty fish that runs clear down the river and under a bridge. Backing is cheap. This day and age, (love saying that), backing is offered in a variety of cool colors so as to enhance the beauty of your reel. Got a purple reel? Maybe get some lime green backing. I personally use dark colors. Here is a diagram for how to get backing onto your reel. You want to be sure the handle is on the left side for right-handed people and on the right side for left handed people. The result has to feed backing out of the bottom of the reel and feed clear of any decorative parts of the reel's aperture.

KNOTS

Backing on the reel (Duncan Loop)

1) Pass the backing from the front of the reel through the line guard and around the arbor twice then back out the front again.

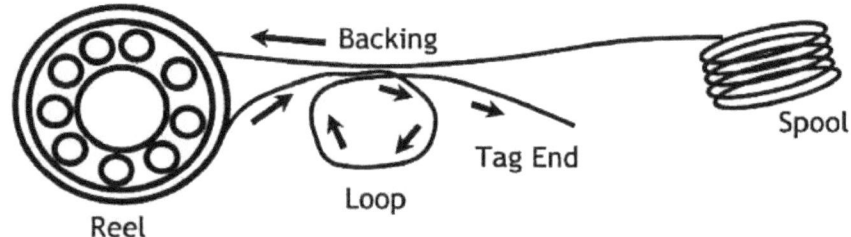

2) Form a loop on the tag end of the backing. Put the top of the loop against the backing that is coming from the spool.

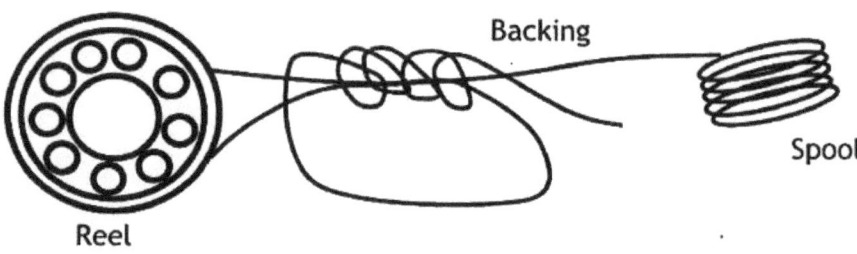

3) Using the tag end, make 4 wraps around the top of the loop and the backing from the spool.

4) Pull the tag end to tighten this slip knot. Trim the tag end (but not flush against the knot).

Note: A lot of backing makes a fatter spool, which makes retrieval go faster. Also, a large trout can run for a long distance with a lot of backing. Backing is cheap. Use a lot of backing.

Figure 45 "Duncan Loop" for tying the backing onto the reel's arbor, (source, Mark Cole, Instructor, Colorado Mountain College, Leadville Campus).

FINAL NOTES

HOW TO CONNECT THE BACKING TO YOUR LINE (PAINFUL)

Your choice here, from most painful to least painful:

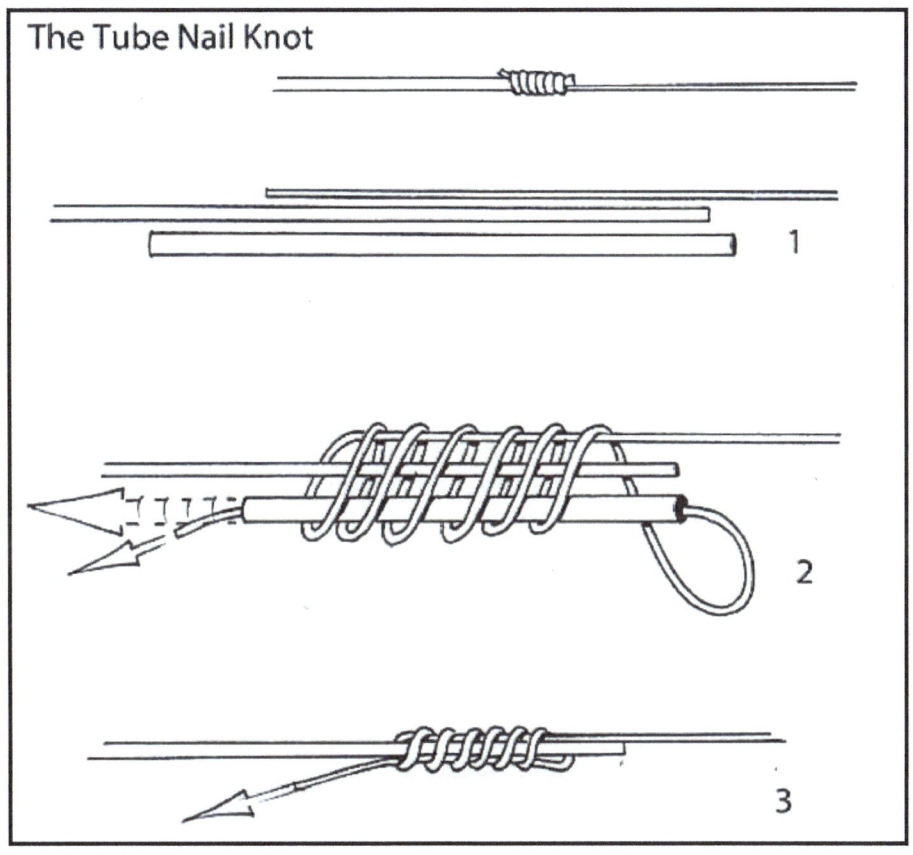

Figure 46 "Tube Nail Knot" for connecting line to backing. I use a straw instead of a nail and I push the tag end through the straw and then pull the straw out of the system. (Source, Mark Cole, Instructor, Colorado Mountain College, Leadville Campus).

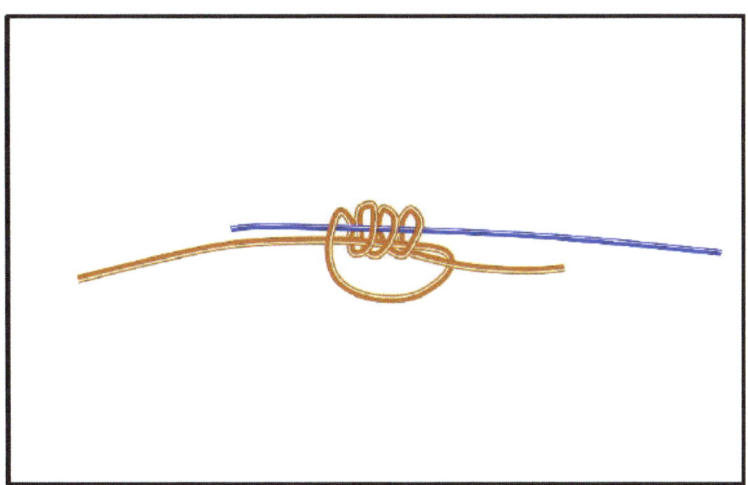

Figure 47 Here is an easy variation for a Lazy Man to tie a nail knot...

FINAL NOTES

How to Connect the Line to the Leader (if you don't have lovely loops to utilize)

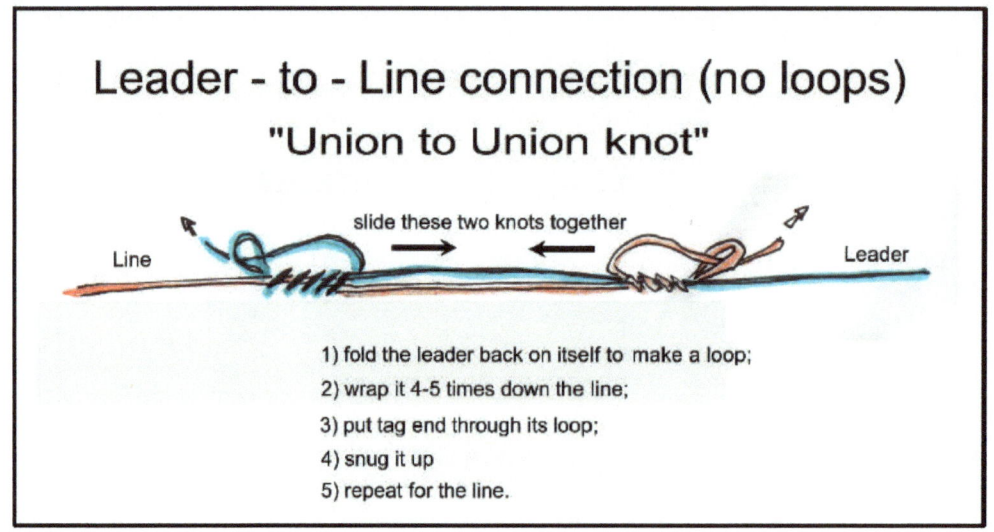

Figure 48 "Union to Union Knot", for leader-to-line connection.

Or, just buy a line that ends in a loop and buy leader that also ends in a loop. Much easier....

Here is the "Davy Wotton Knot" for tying on really little (#24, 26, and smaller) flies:

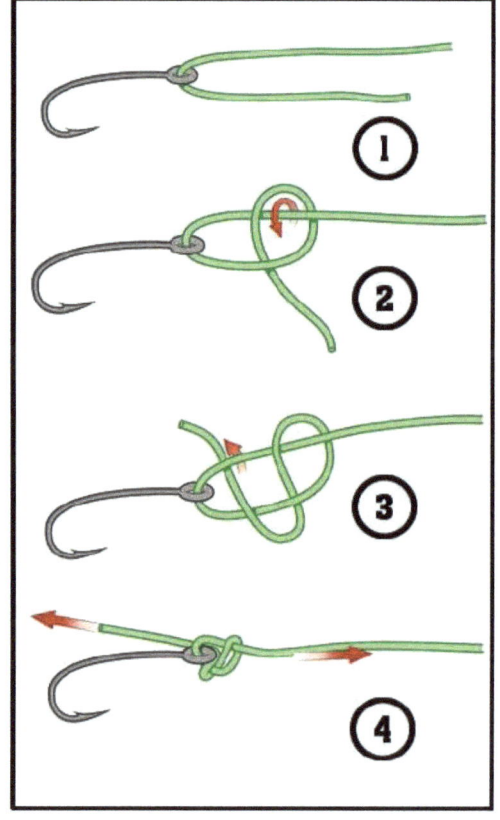

www.ingramcontent.com/pod-product-compliance
Lightning Source LLC
Chambersburg PA
CBHW041432010526
44118CB00002B/53